DICK BIRD 17TH APRIL, 1990.
(ASHES - FLETCHING CHURCHYARD, EAST SUSSEX)

OPERAT

The author, 1945

OPERATION SKUA

Major Richard Thomas Partridge

DSO Royal Marines (Retd)

FRIENDS OF THE FLEET AIR ARM MUSEUM
1983

First published in 1983 by The Fleet Air Arm Museum
Royal Naval Air Station, Yeovilton, Somerset BA22 8HT
for the Society of Friends of the FAA Museum
in association with Picton Publishing (Chippenham) Ltd.

Designed by Colin Huston and Ian Burns
Printed in Great Britain by
AB Printers Limited, Leicester

ISBN 0 902633 86 4

Acknowledgements

'The Skua's recovery', abridged from an original article by Lt A. G. Linsley, RN is
reproduced by kind permission of the editor of *Flightdeck*, the Fleet Air Arm Quarterly.

'The Blackburn Skua described', reprinted from *The Aeroplane*, 9th August 1939 is
reproduced by kind permission of *Flight International*.

Pictures are reproduced by kind permission of the following: Authors collection 2, 13, 15,
17b, 18-19, 18b, 21, 24, 25, 26a/b, 27, 33, 34a/b, 38a, 40, 60, 99, 107, 109, 114, 124, 127,
132, 150; Bergen University Library, picture collection 58a/b, 61b; Ian Burns 29, 32, 65;
Charterhall Productions Ltd 128, 129, 144, 145a/b, 148; Fleet Air Arm Museum 17a, 22,
28a/b, 37, 38b, 42a/b, 48, 53, 54, 66, 68, 71, 75, 80a/b, 82a/b, 159; Sevald Grotli 76, 81, 83;
Imperial War Museum 45, 46, 51, 57a/b, 67, 91a/b, 92, 106, 112, 117; Norsk Telegrambyra
A/S 59; Simon Partridge 150; Portsmouth & Sunderland Newspapers Ltd 149a/b; Skaugstad
Diving & Historical Research, Trondheim 61a.

Contents

Foreword

by the Commandant General Royal Marines
Lieutenant General Sir Steuart R Pringle, Bt

The Royal Marines have been fully involved in military aviation since its earliest days, Lieutenant E L Gerrard being selected in 1910 for duty in No 1 Rigid Airship and in 1912 becoming one of the first instructors at the Central Flying School using his own aearoplane paid for by the Admiralty.

During the First World War thirteen pilots flew with the RNAS and one with the RFC earning between them 9 DSOs, 3 CMGs, 1 CBE and 2 AFCs. On the formation of the RAF in 1918 ten Royal Marines transferred and most subsequently rose to high rank.

During the Second World War forty Royal Marines flew as pilots again covering themselves with honours. Eleven aircraft carriers at various times had Royal Marines in the appointment of Commander (Flying).

Lieutenant C H Collet, on 22 September 1914, had led the first ever bombing raid and Royal Marines were to continue to achieve 'firsts' and break records, including the first ever night deck landing in a single seat aircraft, and the 1934 record from UK to Australia and return.

Major Partridge's story told in this book with great modesty includes an important first of its own in the sinking of a major warship by dive bombers, a lesson not lost on either the United States or Japan. *Operation Skua* imparts a strong flavour of what Naval aviation was like before the last war and during its early days. What it makes little of is the physical strain of operational flying in those days and the severe burns the author suffered and overcame as a result of being shot down.

It is of particular interest to Royal Marines serving today that much of Major Partridge's operational flying took place over the Narvik and Andalsnes areas of Norway where today the light helicopters of 3 Commando Brigade Air Squadron RM train in some of the world's most demanding terrain and weather conditions, thereby continuing the long tradition of flying Marines of which the author of this book is a gallant part.

S R PRINGLE
Lieutenant General

The badge of the Distinguished Service Order

PROLOGUE

Sink or swim...

Robin, my observer, had just said again, 'Me 109s attacking astern and abeam', when I felt a thud that shook my Skua and a large piece, about the size of a soup plate, came away from my starboard wing. It was probably a cannon shell but it was outboard of the ailerons and I still had control of my aircraft. Almost immediately there was another thud and a muffled explosion and the petrol tank behind my instrument panel, only a foot or two from my lap, went up in a roar of flames. From then on my actions were essentially reflex and must have been carried out at lightning speed.

I can remember slamming back my cockpit hood and the resulting slipstream drawing a great sheet of flame up between my legs, across my face and out of the cockpit; I can remember hitting the quick-release of my fighting harness; and then I was at 3500 feet floating down in my parachute with an Me 109 heading straight for me only to swerve aside at the last moment.

As I quickly sank lower I looked desperately around for Robin's parachute but saw only a great fountain of water as my aircraft hit the fjord about a mile ahead of me. All my efforts to guide myself towards the shore of the fjord were failing and I found myself heading slap for the middle.

To avoid being entangled in my parachute in the water I slipped it at about 20 feet above the surface and plummeted down. As the cold waters closed over me I felt a searing pain as the salt came into contact with my burnt face. Then I bobbed to the surface and searched anxiously for shore. From eye level a few inches above the water's surface the land, though only a mile or a mile and a half away, appeared as a distant low misty blur. With my Mae West flotation waistcoat on I knew I was not going to drown but in those cold waters I was also aware that I couldn't last long. Already the conditions were beginning to tell and, save for my face which felt red hot, I could feel the cold penetrating right into my bones.

I turned towards the shore and began to swim slowly with a clumsy breast stroke — I couldn't possibly make it but it seemed better than staying still and slowly dying of cold. After twenty minutes swimming I paused and looked up — the coast line still seemed as far away as ever and I was getting very weak. I was terribly cold and even my face had stopped feeling hot and burning.

I started to swim again, but more slowly now...

1

Growing up

I infuriate my children by still regarding anything that happened after World War II as 'recent'. They were born in 1947 and 1948 so I suppose their point of view is understandable, as is their irritation when I reminisce on such things as a pint of beer at ninepence, a packet of cigarettes for one shilling or a gallon of petrol at one and sixpence. 'Try living in the present Pop', they say, 'and forget about the past'. In spite of this I am encouraged to try and write this book by the fact that they don't seem to tire of tales of my experiences in World War II and in the hope that any reader may find it of interest too.

My mother was clever enough to give birth to me on 10.10.10., the 10th October 1910, and I have always stoutly maintained, quite untruly, that it was at 10 minutes past 10 in the morning, so that my real date of birth is 10.10.10.10.10. We were, I suppose, a middle class family, not upper-middle or lower-middle but middle-middle. The family consisted of my father, a broker on the London Stock Exchange; mother who was one of the large Victorian family of an Exeter estate agent; my sister Marjorie, the eldest of us children and four years older than myself; my brother Paul two years older than me; and lastly, myself, inevitably known initially as 'Little Dick' and remaining that as far as my mother was concerned right up into middle age.

I have always regarded myself as a country person and a non-city dweller, though it didn't start that way. I was born in Hampstead and my very earliest memories at the age of about four and a half are of Queens Road, Richmond where we lived, of walks in Richmond Park, and of World War I soldiers being billetted on us from time to time. All this came to an abrupt end in 1916 when my father decided that mother and the children must leave London to avoid the Zeppelin raids, and we were moved to a very small semi-detached house in West Worthing while father stayed on in London for his work. At that time we three children were aged roughly ten, eight and six and, I suppose as children of that age, were not much affected by war, but for our parents it was a very different kettle of fish. My mother suffered a sudden and severe reduction in her standard of living and was left on her own to bring up three young children. Gone were her nanny, cook and parlour maid and I don't think there was too much money to spare either; none of which really affected us children much, especially me as the youngest.

My memories of those early war days in Worthing are mostly pleasant. We of course had no car but thought nothing of the two mile walk to the beach with our picnic food, nor of the five or six mile walk to High Salvington on the Downs behind Worthing where we used to have tea at the Windmill. A particular treat in the autumn was a train ride to Angmering (about six miles), thence by pony and trap to Angmering Woods where we spent the day blackberrying. They were happy days for kids but I guess worrying and difficult for parents. Only once as a seven year old was the war really brought home to me and that was on the beach one day in 1917. There was a muffled explosion way out at sea and some hours later we saw a ship's boat (it looked huge to me) approaching which pulled up on the shingle right below our beach hut. A lot of men got out carrying another who was struggling and screaming in the most terrible manner. They were the crew of a ship that had been torpedoed and the wounded man had been dreadfully scalded in the engine room. My mother and all of us children were very upset and shocked and I have never forgotten it.

I had been going to school at a kindergarten called Miss Thacker's in Grand Avenue. I only mention this because it was here that I met a little girl called Fay, and it was this little girl whom I married, nearly 30 years later, soon after World War II ended. We had planned to marry before the war but the outbreak of hostilities put a stop to that and we had to wait until August 1946. In case anyone is wondering I hasten to add that we are still happily married and looking forward to our Ruby Wedding in 1986!

My last memory of World War I is of walking along Worthing seafront on Armistice Day waving a Union Jack, but I was still too young to really appreciate the importance of the occasion.

It was six months or so before father rejoined the family. During the first two and a half years of the war he had been a special constable in London, only an occasional and part time job. He was over age for call-up for military duties but in late 1916 he finally volunteered, was accepted, and served in one of the County Regiments as Private Partridge for the rest of the war.

With peace, life began to return to normal and the family fortunes to recover rapidly. We moved from our little semi-detached into quite a large rented house with a big garden and my brother and I were now at a Worthing preparatory school. Father was a senior partner in his well known stockbroking firm and in the boom of the early twenties must have made quite a fortune. At any rate it was large enough, in 1923, for him to announce that he was retiring.

We were now well into the years of peace between the two wars and the family fortunes were to continue to flourish until the Wall Street crash in the early 1930s. In September 1923 my brother and I were sent to Eastbourne College. I was only 12¾ years old, rather young for a public school, but it was thought that we would be company for each other. I managed to survive my first year or two there, but I can remember a shed tear now and then. Public schools were still quite tough in those days!

Father bought a large house in West Worthing and the next seven years were spent in comparative luxury. He also bought a car, a Vauxhall 23/60. This was in the days before General Motors had taken over Vauxhalls, and the days of the great rivalry between the 3 litre Bentley, the 3 litre Sunbeam and the Vauxhall 23/98. Our Vauxhall, a large open tourer, was hand-made and hand-painted by craftsmen and served the family magnificently for 150,000 miles. I can remember our chauffeur, Stanley Hart, having to go to Vauxhalls for a three week's course before we took possession of the car. Many a time this car took the family from Worthing to Cornwall, 256 miles, in eight hours; not bad for over fifty years ago. We were all great Cornwall fans, which stemmed from the fact that my mother and father spent their honeymoon at the Watergate Bay Hotel, a few miles north of Newquay. They fell in love with Cornwall from that moment and we children obviously inherited this love. Every year we used to rent a house on the beach at Porth just north of Newquay for June and August. For many years the family spent happy summer holidays there, in fact until we children grew up and went our separate ways.

Brother Paul and I were working our way through public school and in 1927 he left Eastbourne College for Oxford to read Law. He was there for four years and, although a degree evaded him, he distinguished himself by getting a Tennis Blue and playing for the University for several years. Curiously enough we three children were all good at games; I say curiously because although our parents played some not very good tennis they could not be described as good games players. My sister Marjorie played badminton for Sussex for several years and was an above average tennis player. My brother played tennis for Sussex for many years

The author and cousin almost at sea in a Cornish bay. This raft, named *The Worpor* after the towns Worthing and Porth, was one of two in that area, the other belonging to a friend, Nigel Tangye, who stayed nearby.

13

as well as playing for Oxford, and I was a reasonable tennis, squash, badminton and rugger player.

After my brother left I had two more years at Eastbourne College and ended up as captain of the rugger XV and second Head Boy of School. It was during these two years that I began thinking of a service career, and I find it very difficult to explain why. There was no history of service careers on my father's or mother's side of the family. I think it must have started when I was about 15 and friendly with a boy who was superannuated and whose father was planning to send him to the training ship *Worcester*. This sounded terribly romantic and exciting to me and I immediately wrote to my father asking to be taken away from Eastbourne and sent to *Worcester*. Father had the good sense to stall me and said we would discuss it at Christmas, a good six months ahead, by which time of course I had forgotten all about it. But perhaps this incident had sown the seeds of a desire for a career at sea.

Two years later a the age of 17½ I finally decided that I wanted to join the Navy and it was agreed by my father and the school's career master that I should take the Civil Service Examination for public school entry into the Royal Navy or Royal Marines in the summer of 1928. This was a stiff competitive exam and one's chances varied a lot with the number of vacancies and the number of applicants. One had to state one's preference for the branch of the service and I gave Navy (Executive Branch), Navy (Engineering) and Royal Marines in that order. The exam took place at the Civil Service Commission in London and consisted of three or four days written exams and an interview in front of an interview board, chaired by an Admiral with senior naval and marine officers as members. This interview was no mean ordeal, but was of great importance as it carried a lot of marks and a poor showing could more than cancel out any academic brilliance shown in the written exams.

Suffice to say that I failed to be accepted for any of my choices at my first attempt in the summer of 1928 and was talking to my father about going up to Cambridge to read Engineering. My housemaster then pointed out that there was another Civil Service exam in December for which I was eligible, and he persuaded me to have another try. This time I felt I did better and the terrifying, but all important interview went quite well.

The end of term came on 17th December 1928 when a telegram arrived which read as follows:—

> 'You have been appointed a Probationary Second Lieutenant in the Royal Marines and will report to Captain Phillip Royal Smith-Hill, Royal Marines at the Royal Naval College, Greenwich on the 2nd January 1929.'

My service career was about to begin.

2

I join the Royal Marines

Here, I think, a brief word or two is required about officer entry into the Royal Marines. It differed from the other services inasmuch as there was no cadet training college such as Dartmouth, Sandhurst or Cranwell to attend prior to receiving a commission.

The Royal Marine Officer was commissioned on joining straight from school as a Probationary Acting Second Lieutenant, which, of course, was the lowest form of

The 15th Class of Marines poses for an official portrait during the seamanship course on the battleship *Iron Duke* in 1929. The author is third from left in the middle row.

commissioned life. And there is a lot of significance behind the word 'Probationary', which appendage dogged one for the first four years of service. Briefly what it meant was that if for any reason you were not considered suitable your commission could be abruptly terminated, without any such formality as a Court Martial. One of the batch of six who passed the exam with me in 1928 just disappeared in this way one day after three years — we never did discover why.

To describe our training in full would need a book on its own, which book would contain a lot of funny incidents but also quite a few near-disasters and far from funny where we were concerned. We went from establishment to establishment, Naval, Army and RM, doing courses in naval gunnery, gas warfare, small arms, 15" naval gunnery turret drill, physical training, close order drill, naval mines and torpedoes (and if there was another course the likelihood is that we did it); and believe it or not we also had to be qualified equestrians. Shades of the Horse Marines!

I have never been really good with horses and still regard them with suspicion and distrust. Our riding instruction took place every Friday for the six months that we were at the Naval College, Greenwich. Naval transport used to take us to the Royal Artillery Barracks at Woolwich and deposit us at the riding school. Once inside the school we were at the mercy of a very fierce but very competent gunner sergeant. We were lined up on one side and the horses were led in the other. On the order 'Mount' we doubled across the school, seized a horse and hopefully mounted. After a few weeks we knew the horses pretty well; some were quiet and easy and some were devils. To this day I remember a beautiful little mare called Blue Gown on whom it was almost impossible to do anything wrong; the competition for her was great and two of us desperately trying to mount her at the same time used to provoke some very loud plain speaking from our instructor. I also remember what I considered was a most ill-mannered animal called Tessa, among whose vices was an apparently ungovernable urge to roll in the tan. Many a time I was grovelling on the ground amidst flailing hooves and stentorian shouts of 'Kick her up, SIR, kick her up!' Our instructor must have been good and very patient for he eventually got even me to go down the 'grid' successfully. The grid consisted of a series of jumps and had to be ridden without stirrups and with arms folded.

Late 1932 found me in the RM Barracks, Chatham on general duties having, much to my surprise and relief, successfully completed my training and been promoted to Probationary Lieutenant. You will note that the 'Probationary' was still dogging me. I was now waiting for the next normal step in my career — appointment to a battleship or cruiser as RM subaltern to the RM detachment carried by these ships. After six months in such an appointment, and if recommended as suitable by the captain, I would lose the probationary and become a fully qualified Lieutenant in His Majesty's Corps of Royal Marines.

I didn't have long to wait and one day I found a drafting chit in my letter rack in the Officers Mess telling me that I had been appointed as RM subaltern in HMS *Hermes* on the China Station and that I would take passage in HMS *Vindictive*, a cruiser now lying in Chatham, which would shortly be taking reliefs for the China Fleet to Hong Kong.

This posting turned out to be of the greatest significance for me, for HMS *Hermes*

Nine float-mounted Fairey Flycatchers of 403 (Fleet Fighter) Flight aboard HMS *Hermes* during China Station service in the late 1920s.

was not a battleship or a cruiser, but an aircraft carrier; and it was in this ship that my interest in flying developed, which in turn prompted me to specialize as a pilot. And it is what happened to me as a Fleet Air Arm pilot that provides the real *raison d'être* for this book.

When I joined *Hermes* she was more than half-way through her 2½ years commission on the China Station. As a result I had little more than a year in her before she sailed for England to pay off in Plymouth. But it was a great year for me,

Fairey IIIF of 440 Fleet Spotter Flight landing on HMS *Hermes* near Wei-hai-wei, China Station, 1932.

HMS *Hermes* at Wei-hai-wei in 1932 in the centre of a group including three County Class cruisers, four submarines and the depot ship HMS *Medway*.

exciting and interesting, and, green and inexperienced as I was, I managed to cope reasonably well under the fatherly and watchful eye of my Captain RM who was in charge of the Royal Marine detachment. There can be no better way to see the world than in one of His Majesty's ships. Although I was in China for so short a period I still managed 10 days leave in Peking where I was a guest at the British Embassy: the ship visited Japan, Formosa and the Philippines; and we had a memorable month moored off the bund at Shanghai, surely in those days one of the most exciting and entertaining cities in the world.

During the long trip home at the economical speed of 14 knots I put in a request through the captain to specialize in flying. And I should also mention that during my time in *Hermes* I was recommended for confirmation in the rank of Lieutenant RM and so at long last lost my 'Probationary'.

Back in England once again I took my foreign service leave. It was during this leave that I was informed that my application to fly had been approved and I was appointed to Royal Air Force Station, Leuchars, Fife, Scotland for flying training in September 1933.

My flying career was about to start, and was to last until my retirement in 1950.

Fairey IIIF, Mk IIIB, S1478 of 440 FS Flight taking off from HMS *Hermes*. As the IIIF had no brakes it had to be run up against chocks which have just been pulled clear by the two men lying on the deck. After a run of only six to ten feet the tail is already up; the pilot has applied port rudder and aileron lift to the starboard wing to counter propeller torque. Note the absence of arrester gear, and that the aircraft is being flown with wing folding jury-strut still fitted — a fairly common occurrence!

3

A flying Marine

Before giving a brief account of my flying up to the start of World War II, I must explain the organization of naval flying as it was in those days. All the aircraft and all the ground crews belonged to the Royal Air Force. Of the aircrews, roughly half were RAF officers and the other half Royal Navy officers with the odd Royal Marine officer here and there. One of the results of this awkward arrangement was that all naval flying personnel had to have a RAF commission, and they were granted a temporary one. Hence, when I started flying, I was a Lieutenant RM and a Flying Officer RAF, and later a Captain RM and Flight Lieutenant RAF. A squadron embarked in a carrier might be commanded by a Lieutenant Commander RN or a Squadron Leader RAF, and the senior aviation officer on board, Wing Commander Flying, was always a Wing Commander RAF. This cumbersome arrangement lasted until 1938 when the Navy once again took command of its own flying as in the days of the old Royal Naval Air Service.

The training of non-RAF officers, Royal Naval and Royal Marine for the Fleet Air Arm and Army officers for Army Air Co-operation Squadrons, was carried out at RAF Station Leuchars, not far from St Andrews on the east coast of Fife. Leuchars also catered for the odd officer from foreign countries and, when I was there, there was also a very pleasant little Siamese officer, who coped reasonably well with his flying save that he could never be taught to talk about 'gliding' but always insisted on saying he was in 'neutral'. We thought it was rather descriptive.

But first to get to Leuchars. On 15th September 1933 I said goodbye to my family with wishes of good luck from my father and apprehensive pleas from my mother to 'be careful and not fly too fast'. I first drove my car to Worthing station to pick up my passenger for the long drive (600 miles plus) to Scotland. This passenger was my great friend, Lieutenant F S May, RM, who had joined the Marines at the same time as myself. He had just completed a two year commission in the battleship HMS *Warspite* as subaltern to the RM detachment and, like myself, had applied to specialize in flying. He was the son of a retired Commander RN, living in Portsmouth, and had started his journey by train to meet me at Worthing station. We were both delighted that, purely fortuitously, we were joining up once again, this time to learn to fly.

Francis Stanley May (nick-named 'Tiddler' because he wasn't very tall) and I had been inseparable during our initial three years training in the Marines, and after qualifying as pilots were to serve together again for a couple of years in the Mediterranean in HMS *Glorious* with 802 Squadron.

Tiddler and I had obtained a route from Worthing to Leuchars from the AA and set off on our long drive. What a difference it made to have such an ideal companion; it turned a long and tedious journey, with my usual apprehensions about joining a new and strange establishment, into an enjoyable adventure. We thundered up the A1 (no motorways in those days) in my 20 hp Rover open two-seater and after about 5½ hours found ourselves running through a very drab Doncaster. That meant about 200 miles gone and another 400 to go!

Tiddler was keeping a log of the journey which was beginning to get full of entries like: 'Stopped to let off steam — half pint at Three Crowns — half at White Hart — half pint at etc., etc.' until fortunately closing time put a stop to half pints. About 100 miles further on we were looking for a place to stop for the night and keeping left at Scotch Corner onto the A66, we shortly afterwards turned off to Barnard Castle to spend the night at a cheap and rather indifferent pub, not that that worried us much at the age of 23.

We were up early next morning with about 300 miles to go. A lovely drive across the Yorkshire Moors, now on the A68, we kept south and west of Edinburgh to cross the Firth of Forth by ferry at South Queensferry (there was no road bridge then). We were now on the last lap of our journey with about 50 miles to go. We went through strange sounding (to us) places like Kirkcaldy, Craigrothie, Cupar and Dairsie to arrive at RAF Station, Leuchars in the early evening.

The author in his Sidcot suit, Leuchars 1934   **F S 'Tiddler' May**

Avro 504N, K1988 inverted (though not by the author) at No. 1 Flying Training School, Leuchars, 1934.

It is 47 years ago now that I first set eyes on Leuchars and I have not been back since I completed my flying training. Memories dim but first impressions seem to endure. I can well recall the Officers Mess set just across the road running alongside the airfield, a collection of single storey buildings rather suggestive of World War I army huts. But it was comfortable and adequate inside and had an atmosphere of casual informality very different from others I had been in. Tiddler and I were received in a friendly manner and, finding quite a number of naval officers we had met or served with before, we soon settled in.

Having been in the Service for nearly five years by now we were well acquainted with Naval, Marine and Army Messes and establishments. The RAF, however, was new ground to us and we found that the informality in the Mess was to run through-out the station and was all very easy-going. I don't think any of us 'pupils' from different services took advantage of the easier circumstances we found ourselves in, though I do remember one naval officer who used to wander down to the hangars after breakfast under an open umbrella on rainy days. When questioned he stoutly maintained it was accepted practice in naval barracks!

At any rate we were here to learn to fly and I found the flying instruction first class, as I think did the others. The Flying Training Squadron was divided into Flights A, B and C: 'A' Flight carried out elementary training lasting three months; 'B' Flight gave us three months intermediate training on more advanced aircraft; and 'C' gave us three months operational training on the aircraft we were going to fly in the Navy. So, in all, with leave, our course lasted a year and there were always three batches of pupils at different stages of training. This made a total pupil population of 40-50 officers, mostly naval.

My course consisted of two Royal Marine officers, Tiddler and myself, about ten Navy officers and three Army officers. We were a mixed bunch, ranging from the wild dashing extrovert to the quiet meditative loner and I think that somewhere in the middle of those extremes you would have found me. In spite of these varying temperaments and personalities Leuchars managed to turn us all out as qualified pilots, which speaks highly for the standard of flying training we received.

We were all a little apprehensive as to how we would react to flying, but our introduction on the first day was so gentle and understanding that I think most of us were quickly reassured. First came the issue of flying clothing which consisted of flying helmet, with ear-pieces and Gosport tubing for inter-cockpit communication; woolly-lined flying boots; Sidcot suit with detachable teddy-bear lining; large leather gauntlets with white silk gloves to wear underneath; and finally a parachute. With all this equipment on it was hardly possible to move but it was very welcome in unheated open cockpits at 10,000 feet on a bitter Scottish winter's day. Next we were shown the aircraft that we would be flying for the next three months of our initial training, the Avro 504N. I think anybody could be forgiven for assuming that it was a relic of World War I, and it very nearly was. Surprisingly, it was really quite a good aircraft to learn on; it had no vices and was very basic, with a minimum of cockpit instruments, just air speed indicator, turn and bank indicator and altimeter. It had dual controls of course and after a time we all got rather fond of it.

Now we were ready for our first flight with our instructors who had assured us that it would be a gentle flight with no aerobatics unless we asked for them. The commander of 'A' Flight was a gay and dashing Flight Lieutenant who went by the nickname of SAP, not very complimentary, but an abbreviation of his full and even less polite nickname of Split-Arse Pete. In spite of all this he was a magnificent pilot and a first rate instructor. I trained under him for my first two days but I think he must have got fed up with me as I was passed on to a quiet and competent flying officer instructor with whom I remained to complete the initial three months training.

Two things remain firmly fixed in my mind after all these years — my initial familiarization flight with Split-Arse Pete and of course my first solo. In my first flight it was the flimsiness of the Avro that impressed me so much; it was just fabric, wires and wood that separated me from the little square fields below. But I was enjoying the gentle turns, dives and climbs and with mounting confidence was just deciding that this was the life for me when SA Pete obviously couldn't resist asking me if I would like to do a loop. Not being brave enough to retort — 'You must be joking!' — I replied a feeble 'Yes' and survived my first view of the world upside down.

I doubt if there are any pilots, however old and experienced, who have forgotten their first solo; it surely must be one of the landmarks of a flying career. I had amassed the great total of 13 hrs 45 mins dual instruction when one morning my instructor told me the Flight Commander was going to give me a test to assess my progress. At Leuchars the pupil occupied the rear cockpit and the instructor the front and after SA Pete had climbed in in front of me I was told to taxi out and take off. I flew around for ten minutes doing gentle turns, steep turns and various normal manoeuvres until told to land. Having landed and taxied back for another take-off Pete said 'Hang on a moment' and climbed out of his cockpit, leaving a horrible empty space in front instead of the back view of a really competent and experienced instructor.

'You're OK to go solo', I was told. 'Just take off, fly around for ten minutes, then land and taxi to the hangars'. With that Pete turned his back and walked away to his flight office.

The moment of truth had arrived. Gingerly I eased the throttle forward and as speed over the ground built up, remembering all I had been taught, I eased the stick forward to get the tail up, kept the aircraft reasonably straight and then easing back on the stick found myself airborne with this horrible empty cockpit in front of me! Flying around at 2-3000 feet in sight of the aerodrome was easy and I was beginning to enjoy myself whilst trying to forget that the most difficult part was to come — landing with many critical eyes watching me. As I swung round in a left-hand turn for my final approach to the airfield, I was concentrating too hard to be frightened and flattening out at the correct height and speed, surprised myself by making a very good three point landing. As I taxied back towards the tarmac in triumph, I realized that I was sweating and a little shaky from the intense concentration I had given to my first solo. The verdict from my Flight Commander and my instructor was a quiet and casual 'Well done, you made a very nice landing'. I was elated as I walked back to the Mess for lunch.

I realize now that it is only one's own first solo that is such a momentous occasion. All the pupils in my batch were successful after various periods of dual instruction, ranging from 10 to 16 hours and, curiously, it wasn't always the first to succeed who turned out eventually to be the best pilots.

Round about the middle of December, we had all done 27 hours dual and 29 hours solo and our initial training in 'A' Flight was completed. We were assessed for competence and I was more than happy to find that I was deemed 'above average'; and even happier to find that we now had four weeks Christmas leave.

Inexplicably, Tiddler May and I decided to do the drive south in one go! Looking back on it, after all these years, I think we must have been mad, especially when I call to mind some of the fine hotels and pubs we passed, such as the Three Arrows at Boroughbridge in Yorkshire with its lovely bedrooms, not numbered but called the Mauve Room, Pink Room, Yellow Room etc. It was of course the exuberance of youth and a challenge to be met and conquered. But challenge or no challenge, we had a rotten time and never tried it again.

Bristol Bulldog TM, K3175 a two-seat training version of the famous single-seat fighter.

We left Leuchars at 1.30 pm and arrived at Worthing for breakfast at 9 am the following morning, having survived snow, ice and fog over the Yorkshire moors; having been pulled out of a slippery ditch by friendly lorry drivers and having got incredibly cold in an unheated car. We arrived stiff, cold and hungry — talk about banging your head against a wall because it's so nice when you stop. I can remember being taken to the cinema in Brighton by my family that same afternoon and sleeping through the whole performance, much to their annoyance.

After Christmas we were back at Leuchars again, this time to join 'B' Flight for our next stage of flying training. 'B' Flight had a varied collection of aircraft — a dual version Bristol Bulldog; a dual Hawker Hart; a Hawker Osprey (the naval version of the Hart); a single seat Fairey Flycatcher; and we still had the Avro 504N, but for instrument flying training only. Of these aircraft my favourite was the Bulldog. Not only was it nice to look at but it was a delight to fly and would almost land itself in a perfect three pointer; that is wheels and tailskid all touching down at exactly the same time. Our flying was getting more advanced now and included such things as aerobatics; solo cross country flights to nearby aerodromes at Abbotsinch and Aberdeen; rough weather flying; height tests and cloud flying. As far as I remember, we did about 17 hours dual and 33 hours solo in 'B' Flight and all went well with all of us. I had just one minor scare when, solo in a Bulldog, the throttle jammed wide open. I had to return to the aerodrome, cut my engine and make a forced landing with a dead prop. Not really very difficult, but it frightened me a little at the time and I was very glad that it happened when I was flying my favourite Bulldog.

It was now that we were divided into fighter pilots or torpedo bomber pilots. Competition to be the former was keen and usually over-subscribed, though there were those who opted for torpedo bombers in preference. Generally speaking the

Fairey IIIF, S1169 flown several times by the author during 'C' Flight training in July 1934.

'Tiddler' May alongside a Fairey Flycatcher of 1 Flying Training School. The aircraft is fully equipped for night flying with wingtip centre-section and rudder lights, also Holt flares for illuminating night landings.

The Flycatcher was the FAA main fighter from 1923 to 1934 and was one of the few types to be designed from the outset as a Naval aircraft. It could operate on wheels and floats as well as being catapulted if necessary.

The author in front of Hawker Osprey I, S1692 at RAF Leuchars. The Osprey was a naval version of the RAF Hawker Hart day bomber. It replaced the Fairey IIIF and Seal in Fleet Air Arm Spotter Reconnaissance.

fighter pilots were chosen from those who had shown most promise during the past six months flying training and I am happy to say that both Tiddler May and I made the grade. We and the other selected fighter pilots would return to complete our training in 'C' Flight at Leuchars, while the torpedo bomber pilots would leave Leuchars to carry out their final three months at RAF Station, Gosport.

With our 'B' Flight training completed in the middle of April 1934, we were off on leave again for four weeks before starting our final three months operational training either at Leuchars or at Gosport. Looking back on it, we seemed to do very well for leave and I departed happily south once again in my car with another 'above average' flying assessment behind me.

'C' Flight was commanded by a quiet and pleasant senior Flight Lieutenant. To us he seemed quite old, being at least in his middle thirties. Like most of the instructional flying staff at Leuchars he was very competent both as an instructor and as a pilot. We were now starting the advanced and most varied part of our course which was to include ADDLs (Aerodrome Dummy Deck Landings), aerobatics, formation flying, bombing and front gun firing on the nearby armament ranges, and catapult launches. In addition to all this, in the middle of the course we all went to RAF Calshot, the flying-boat and seaplane base near Southampton, to do a week's flying in seaplanes.

We were now flying mostly aircraft that were in service with the Fleet Air Arm, the three-seater spotter reconnaissance Fairey IIIF and Seal, the single-seat naval fighter the Hawker Nimrod and the two-seat Hawker Osprey. None of these aircraft were designed for naval work but were conversions of existing RAF types. The Nimrod corresponded to the RAF Fury and the Osprey to the Hart. The trouble

Hawker Nimrod ready for take-off after being crane-mounted onto the catapult at RAF Leuchars. Just prior to launch the pilot would open the throttle and the acceleration of the catapult, combined with the thrust of the propeller, produced the required flying speed. The trolley automatically stopped at the end of the catapult runway as the aeroplane was released.

with these conversions was that by the time such gear as arrestor hooks and flotation equipment had been added, performance had also been considerably reduced. The Nimrod was to remain the Fleet Air Arm's fighter aircraft until replaced by the Blackburn Skua at the end of 1938, by which time it was completely outclassed by the fighters of other nations. I was to fly many hundreds of hours in Nimrods and Ospreys until the Skua arrived.

The float-plane course at Calshot made a pleasant week's break in the middle of our final three months training. I completed 1 hr 40 mins dual in a Fairey Seal, followed by 4 hrs 10 mins solo in the same type of aircraft. I also had 15 minutes dual in an Avro Tutor on floats; I can't remember why. The Tutor was a small two-seat training aircraft, quite pleasant to fly but grossly underpowered when flying with two large floats. On still days, when the water was glassy, it was very difficult to get the aircraft unstuck and airborne, and it was quite common to see a pilot taxying round on very calm days until he found the wake from a power boat or ship. He would then take off across the ripples caused by the wake, the disturbed water helping the aircraft to get in the air. I enjoyed my float-plane course, and it was to come in very useful later on when I did a fair amount of flying in Ospreys with floats.

My catapult launch training at Leuchars still remains firmly fixed in my mind, as in those days the catapult was operated by a cordite charge, so one really was fired off! Later these catapults were superseded by accelerators, operated at first by compressed air and then by steam. I started with an instructed launch in a Fairey IIIF, followed by three solo launches in the single-seater Nimrod. I well remember that first Nimrod launch, sitting in the cockpit with full revs, hand on the control column with elbow jammed into my side so that it would not jerk back, head hard back against the headrest so that I wouldn't break my neck, raising my left hand to show that I was ready: then BANG — and I was flying away from the aerodrome.

This rear view of the catapult launch at RAF Leuchars clearly shows the single track turntable on which the aircraft would be rotated to make certain it took off into wind.

So far I have only spoken of flying at Leuchars, but obviously we didn't fly all the time, we had to have time off for recreation and social activities. The station ran a very keen and quite good Rugger XV for which I used to play. Most of our fixtures were against other local clubs in that area of Scotland and most winter Saturday afternoons included a rugger match at home or away. We also took part in the RAF inter-unit rugger competition and flew all the way south to play against RAF Hornchurch, some 17 miles east of London, only to get beaten there in the first round. It was however excellent cross-country flying practice for us. My other great sporting love was golf and many a round I played on the Eden Course at St Andrews where the green fee in those days was the princely sum of 1/6 (or in our new currency, 7½ pence). Frequently on a summer Sunday four of us used to drive over to Gleneagles, about 50 miles away, and have a grand day's golf on the lovely Queen's Course there. We couldn't afford to go anywhere near the very luxurious Gleneagles Hotel but used to enjoy a picnic lunch in idyllic surroundings. When there wasn't time for golf, Tiddler May and I had many a hard-fought singles on the tennis courts behind the Officers Mess.

My memories of our social life at Leuchars are extremely scanty and I don't think we had very much. St Andrews was our local town but the number of girls there, at the right sort of age for us, was very limited so the competition was extremely keen. Scattered about the surrounding countryside were some fine great Scottish mansions with young families but not all that number of invitations. I can remember meeting a very attractive girl at a rather rare private dance in St Andrews whose family lived near Perth. After I had danced with her several times, I asked her if she would like to come out to dinner with me the following week. It seemed a harmless enough invitation and her reply really shook me — 'It is out of the question. My parents would never allow me to go out alone with a young officer from Leuchars, and none of my friends are allowed to either'. This of course was the sudden end to what might have been a budding romance! Obviously in some quarters Leuchars did not have a very good name, though during my year there I never saw any behaviour that merited such a reputation.

My only other enduring memory of St Andrews was 'Betty's Bar' in one of the pubs. This was our usual assembly place for the odd drink or two away from the Mess. 'Betty's Bar' was first drawn to my attention in the address the chief flying instructor, a Wing Commander, gave to us newly arrived pupils. 'You won't hurt yourselves flying here but for God's sake be careful driving back on a dark winter's night from 'Betty's Bar',' is what he said.

On 22nd August 1934 I completed my last training flight at Leuchars leading a formation of three Nimrods. My course was finished and I was now a qualified pilot with an assessment of 'above the average'. I was very proud of this assessment; it gave me the opportunity of choosing whether I wanted to be a fleet fighter or reconnaissance torpedo bomber pilot, and in those heady, youthful days I had no hesitation in choosing fighters, but there was still quite a disturbing hurdle to be passed — deck landing.

My early Service career

The aircraft carrier HMS *Courageous* had arrived in the Firth of Forth and there Tiddler May and I embarked to join 802 Squadron. A day or two later the ship sailed to carry out general flying practice which would include the qualifying first landings of May and Partridge. First we had to do four dual landings with a qualified instructor from Leuchars in, of all things, an Avro 504N! As the Avro had a landing speed as low as 45 knots, with no brakes or arrestor hook, deck landing in one bore little resemblance to doing so in a Nimrod. Additionally, the instructor (Split-Arse Pete again in my case) sat in the front cockpit and the pupil in the rear. Consequently on the most important part of the landing, the final approach, the pupil could see little or nothing of the carrier's deck but a lot of the instructor's back. Of course one did get an idea of what the carrier looked like from the air, especially on the turn in for the final approach!

Deck landing training on HMS *Glorious* being carried out in the ever popular Avro 504N

I did my four landings with SA Pete and he made it look so easy, touching down gently each time in perfect three point landings. Then I found myself on the after end of the flight deck in a Nimrod, ready to go it alone, with instructions to do four take-offs and landings. Tiddler May had gone before me and I had watched him do four very good landings. Offering up a silent prayer, I eased the throttle forward and took off.

My four qualifying landings went very well. I was vastly relieved, surprised and jubilant; almost as jubilant as I was after my first solo. But there was trouble to come and for a time my confidence was to be severely shaken. Four days after my qualifying landings, *Courageous* was at sea once again for general flying. I was sent up in my Nimrod to carry out an R/T test and all went well until I returned to the ship. On landing, I came in too high and too slow, dropped a wing, slewed sharply to starboard and crashed into the pallisades, which were protective wire netting and supports running down each side of the flight deck to stop such bad landings as mine from going over the side. My aircraft was damaged but all I suffered was a blow to my pride and confidence.

Three days later, I was sent up again to carry out six take-offs and landings and all went well until my sixth and final approach when, coming in too fast with tail up, I caught a wire, tipped forward and shattered the end of my propeller on the deck. So much for my 'above average' assessment. It was now touch and go whether I would be retained by 802 Squadron and I was sent back to Leuchars for two days to carry out intensive flying practice including ADDLs. A few days later I returned to *Courageous,* carried out four very good landings, and I am glad to say that I never again had a deck landing accident. But it was a trying period for me and certainly taught me never to be over-confident where matters of flying were concerned.

HMS *Courageous* off Gibralter about 1930. A Fairey IIIF appears on the forward part of the deck: several Blackburn Darts of 463/464 Flights are ranged aft.

The author flying Hawker Nimrod I, K2834 of 802 FF Squadron at Netheravon, 1935. The aircraft is equipped for night flying and carries a camera gun on the starboard lower wing.

Classic inter-war view of three Nimrods of 802 Squadron practising formation flying for the Royal Review of the Fleet, Netheravon 1935.

I was now appointed to 802 Squadron at RAF Station Netheravon, on Salisbury Plain, where the next year was spent hard at work, getting a lot of flying and working the squadron up to a state of high efficiency. It was during this period that we took part in a historic event — the Fleet Air Arm fly-past at the Royal Naval Review on the 16th July 1935. We put up squadron after squadron of aircraft, I cannot now remember how many, and the vast array of ships large and small stretched for miles; so far in fact that it took us quite some time to fly over them. It was a great sight and it is sad to think that its like will probably never be seen again.

I enjoyed being at Netheravon but my stay there was to come to an abrupt end. In the second half of August 1935 I had just started two weeks leave and was away down in Cornwall, playing in the tennis tournament at Bude. As I came off the courts, having won my first round in the open singles, I was handed a telegram which read 'Report back 802 Netheravon forthwith'. Within two days the squadron was embarked in HMS *Glorious* and heading full speed for the Mediterranean. Italy had invaded Ethiopa.

The ship remained at Alexandria until April of the next year, during much of which time 802 Squadron was disembarked at Aboukir or Amyria. For the first month or two of the emergency leave was restricted and the squadron had to be at readiness to re-embark at short notice. As things gradually returned to normal, restrictions were eased and then lifted so that once again we were able to sample the delights of Alexandria itself. Late in April *Glorious* sailed for Malta and we resumed a normal peace-time commission in the Mediterranean.

Fairey Seal, K3515 of 823 FS Squadron flying from HMS *Glorious,* with destroyer in rear, off Alexandria about 1935. The Seal was an updated version of the Fairey IIIF, which it superseded in service. The last Seals were retired from RAF service in April 1942, although the Fleet Air Arm replaced them with the Fairey Swordfish in 1938.

The author comes to grief — Hawker Nimrod I, S1634 restrained by the palisades after an awkward landing!

Hawker Osprey III, K3643 of 802 FF Squadron, HMS *Glorious*. The two-seat Ospreys acted as navigation leaders for the single-seat Hawker Nimrod fighters.

Hawker Nimrod I, S1634 of 802 FF Squadron. Note the camera gun fitted above the lower starboard wing. The Nimrod was essentially a naval version of the RAF's Fury fighter with increased wingspan. It was in front line service from 1931 to 1939 and was finally declared obsolete in July 1941.

In May 1936 *Glorious* returned to Alexandria on a routine visit, but within a month my enjoyable time in the Mediterranean was rudely interrupted. A signal arrived from the Admiralty appointing me to HMS *Hermes* once again, this time not as subaltern to the Marine detachment, but as a pilot in 803 Squadron which was equipped with two-seater Hawker Ospreys. I was sorry to be leaving 802 Squadron, *Glorious* and the Mediterranean, but at the same time excited at the thought of returning to China. First though I had to get to *Hermes* which would be in either Hong Kong or Shanghai.

I started off by train from Alexandria for Port Said, the first time I had travelled in an Egyptian train, and very good it was too. At Port Said I was given a first-class passage in the *Kaiser-i-Hind,* the last of the P&O coal-burners, sailing to the Far East, including Hong Kong and Shanghai. If *Hermes* was at Shanghai this would mean a trip of six weeks, and though I was travelling in great comfort I thought it might get boring after a week or two; and it did! I was honoured by being seated at the Captain's table, but whilst appreciating this honour had to watch my step as the Captain was of the old school and a very strict disciplinarian — woe betide anyone who was late for dinner, especially young Marine officers! Indeed there was another Marine officer on board taking passage to Singapore, a very young, good-looking Lieutenant, junior even to me. He took a fancy to a devastatingly attractive half-caste girl travelling steerage and he used to slip aft and chat her up. The Captain found out about this, sent for the young Lieutenant and informed him that he would not tolerate fraternization between his first-class and steerage passengers, and that if it happened again he would be put ashore. Unfortunately, the young Lieutenant either couldn't or wouldn't resist the charms of this girl, and sure enough the Captain kept his word, and he found himself put ashore, bag and baggage, at Aden of all places. I kept strictly away from the steerage and made do quite happily with what the first class had to offer!

About this time it came as a great blow to me to learn that 'Tiddler' May had been killed in a flying accident in Malta. Apparently he had taken off from RAF Station Hal Far to engine-test a Nimrod, and soon after becoming airborne had had engine failure. Malta was a terrible place for a forced landing if it was impossible to reach the sea. It had just the one aerodrome in those days and the surrounding country was divided up into little fields with stone walls. Not being high enough to bale out, Tiddler tried to turn back to the aerodrome and crashed. Sadly he left a young widow who was the All England Ladies Singles Badminton champion, and a most charming girl.

We arrived at Hong Kong: no *Hermes,* but she was reported to be at Shanghai, so I stayed in the *Kaiser-i-Hind* and sailed on. We arrived at Shanghai: still no *Hermes,* and as the *Kaiser-i-Hind* was turning round to sail back to England, I went ashore and appealed to the Resident Naval Officer for help. He said that *Hermes* was at Tsing-Tao, way up north, and arranged for me to stay at the palatial Cathay Hotel until he could book a passage for me to Tsing-Tao in a coastal steamer; he also gave me an advance of pay of which I was in desperate need. Two days later I embarked in my coaster, again first class, but hardly up to P&O standards. After four days we sailed into Tsing-Tao — no *Hermes*! But there was a cruiser, one of our five County Class cruisers which formed the backbone of the China Fleet; I think it was HMS

Cumberland. It was a pleasant change to be in naval company once again with no half-caste girls to tempt one. But my stay was to be very brief as I was told that *Cumberland* was sailing next morning, that *Hermes* was expected and I would have to wait for her ashore. So ashore I went again to the best and biggest hotel on the waterfront. Tsing-Tao was a delightful place with quite a large American colony and some English residents. I was soon having a marvellous time, playing tennis at the American Club, having lunch there and dinner here, dancing, picnicking, swimming and enjoying great hospitality all round. It came as a bit of a shock on the fourth morning to see a strange superstructure rising above the distant horizon — *Hermes*. Once again I was to join the ship towards the end of her commission. I embarked at Tsing-Tao in August 1936 and *Hermes* was to be back home by early May 1937.

Although to date most of my flying had been done in single-seater Nimrods, I had flown the two-seater Osprey before and was reasonably familiar with it; it had the advantage of a much increased endurance and it could also be put onto floats and so converted into a seaplane. This latter advantage was of importance when the China Fleet moved from Hong Kong to its cooler, northern summer base at Wei-hai-wei, where it stayed for the best part of six months. There was no aerodrome at Wei-hai-wei so we could only fly when *Hermes* was at sea, thus limiting appreciably the number of flying hours we could put in. But by putting two or three Ospreys onto floats we were able to keep in reasonable flying practice without excessive sea-time for the ship.

Osprey I, S1696 of 803 Squadron flying past HMS *Hermes* off Wei-hai-wei, China in 1935. The author flew this floatplane on several occasions during 1936/37.

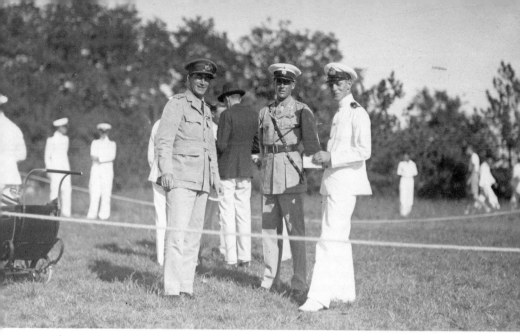

An assortment of uniforms at Wei-hai-wei Sports in 1936. The author in Marine uniform is flanked by Royal Air Force and Navy officers.

Hawker Osprey III floatplane, K3652 of 802 FF Squadron. This shows the result of a landing accident, for which the author was not responsible.

At the end of the summer we sailed south to return to Hong Kong, and on arrival the squadrons were flown off to the RAF station at Kai Tak. There we would normally spend the winter but this time *Hermes* sailed, soon after the New Year, to spend three months at Singapore on the way back to England. We did some flying from the ship whilst on passage to Singapore and on arrival we flew off to the RAF station at Seletar. We had some interesting flying whilst at Singapore.

On 19th February 1937 803 Squadron took off from Seletar at 0640 and landed at Kuala Lumpur at 0820 where we had breakfast; we left Kuala Lumpur again at 1020 and reached Penang at 1150. There was a reason for this long flight up to the north of the Malay Peninsula; we were going to show the flag at the Penang Flying Club's Air Display. We had one Osprey taking part in the fly-past of each type of aircraft there, but the highlight of the show was a display of formation aerobatics by three Ospreys from our squadron. Three of us had been practising for weeks and on the day managed to put on a display that was greeted with tumultuous applause. The sub-flight of three was led by Commander Byas RN, (our Squadron CO) with Flight Lieutenant R S Ryan RAF flying on his right and myself, a Royal Marine officer on his left; a very mixed bunch, but typical of the Fleet Air Arm at that time. Penang was a beautiful place and we were nearly overwhelmed with hospitality. Three days later we returned to Singapore, by an interesting route which included landings at Alor Star, Taiping and Batu Pahar.

Our stay in Singapore was coming to an end and on 10th March 1937 we took off from the RAF station at Seletar and landed on *Hermes* for passage back to the United Kingdom. There was no flying for us on the passage home and for me, a pilot now, there was to be no ceremonial sailing into Plymouth harbour with paying off pennant flying. At 0810 on the morning of 3rd May 1937 *Hermes* flew off her squadrons and proceeded into harbour. We landed at Roborough aerodrome just outside Plymouth, re-fuelled and proceeded to Gosport for our foreign service leave. This was completed by early summer 1937 and although I didn't realize it at the time the war clouds were already beginning to boil up and it was not to be very long before all my varied flying experiences and training would be put to the final test of actual warfare.

The next four months were spent at RAF Station Gosport in a 'pool' of qualified pilots awaiting appointment to squadrons and I was employed on various miscellaneous flying duties as the need arose. Often it was to ferry aircraft of various types from one station to another, and several times I found myself collecting new Blackburn Shark aircraft from their factory at Brough in Yorkshire. But in October 1937 I was appointed to RAF Calshot for a conversion course to the Supermarine Walrus, a single-engined amphibian aircraft which was carried by some cruisers and launched by catapult. With my previous float-plane experience I had no difficulty in completing this course which I found most enjoyable. But whilst waiting for a posting to a cruiser, hopefully on the West Indies Station, I found myself appointed to 802 Squadron once again, as a Flight Commander, and in February 1938 I was on board *Glorious* heading for Malta.

Royal Marine officers who specialized in flying normally had to return to the corps after five years with the Fleet Air Arm for a spell of two years general Royal Marine duties. After that they might return for a further five years flying.

HMS *Glorious*

Accordingly, in October 1938 I was appointed to the Royal Marine Barracks, Plymouth and left *Glorious* and the Mediterranean in a troopship for England.

At this time the storm clouds of war were not only boiling up but beginning to appear above the horizon and it was realized that if war did break out experienced and qualified aircrew would be at a premium. By now I had five years extensive and varied flying experience and in May 1939 a signal arrived at the RM Barracks saying that Captain R T Partridge RM was to be returned to flying duties forthwith. When war was declared on 3rd September 1939 I found myself at the Royal Naval Air Station Eastleigh as a pilot, and I never did return to RM duties.

5

War is declared

3rd September 1939 — we were at war; the Prime Minister had just said so, but nothing happened. This at first was rather baffling and later extremely boring. When at war you expect to fight, but service life for us at Eastleigh continued much the same except that our freedom was greatly restricted; we had no petrol for our cars and we had to wear uniform the whole time. This was the beginning of the period called by the Americans, I believe, the 'phoney war'. For some it lasted months but not for me: before Christmas my war was becoming far from phoney and at times unpleasantly real and hazardous.

September and October were spent at Eastleigh flying mainly Hawker Ospreys and giving the rear gunners air firing practice. Towards the end of October however the new fleet fighter/dive-bombers began to arrive at Eastleigh and we were all soon busy familiarizing ourselves with a very new type of aircraft. As a naval fighter it had several revolutionary features — it was a monoplane, it had a retractable under-carriage, a variable pitch propeller, and it had large and very powerful flaps. As a two-seater it carried a pilot and observer or air gunner.

This aircraft, the Blackburn Skua, was the type that I was chiefly to fly from now until the end of my war career. In spite of its new features we found it an easy aircraft to handle and we soon evaluated it as a first-class dive-bomber, but it was sadly lacking in speed and performance as a fighter. It also tended to be unstable fore and aft when carrying its full ammunition load for the four Browning machine guns in the wings and the Vickers in the rear cockpit, plus one 500 lb and eight 20 lb bombs and petrol for full range of 4½ hours flying. It wasn't many months before I was personally to find out how true this first impression of the Skua was, in both its dive-bombing and fighter capabilities.

Returning one Sunday evening from a brief and rare weekend leave I found that, in addition to my flying duties, I had been appointed station Passive Defence Officer! I had no idea what this meant but I was given a 3rd officer Wren as secretary to help me carry out this added task. She was a charming and pretty young girl but had even less idea of passive defence on a naval air station than I had. It was a case of the blind leading the blind but, as so often happens when confronted with an impossible task, one gets down to it and eventually, after much work and worry, the impossible is achieved. Within a month we had completed a quite comprehen-

Blackburn Shark III, K8901 of the Target Towing Unit, Gosport, early 1940. Whilst the author was flying trainee gunners in Ospreys, Sharks were towing drogues for them to shoot at. This type saw only brief front line service with the FAA from 1935 to 1938, but continued in second line service until 1944.

Blackburn Skuas outside the factory at Brough. On the outbreak of war the Skua was the most modern aircraft in the Fleet Air Arm inventory, although sadly inferior to its land-based contemporaries. The Skua entered front line service in November 1938 and after a brief but glorious career was retired to second line duties in August 1941.

sive manual, laying out the rules and regulations for dispersal of aircraft and transport, construction and allotting of air-raid shelters, manning of light automatic defence guns, and drill and protection against gas attack, etc. This manual was submitted to FO (Air) at RNAS Lee-on-Solent and approved. I also managed to fly most days, training rear gunners to fire at drogue targets towed over the sea, usually off the coast at Littlehampton. It was not very interesting but at least it helped in getting really familiarized and competent with the Skua. I can remember to this day the mnemonic I was given for the essential drill for landing and take-off: PUF and REPUF; that was P for pitch, U for undercarriage, F for flaps, R for rudder trim and E for elevator trim. It seems funny now but you must remember we had never flown anything with retractable undercarriages and variable pitch propellers before.

The 'phoney' war was still on as far as we were concerned and we found the wearing of uniform at all times very restricting; a Southampton pub crawl had to be conducted with unaccustomed decorum. Exercise, which had always had a great attraction for me, also presented problems. The station had no squash or tennis courts and we were not exactly surrounded by good walking country like many of the air stations on say, Salisbury Plain. We did manage to get the odd game of tennis at the Eastleigh public courts until, to my delight, a retired admiral, with a lovely country house nearby, put his own tennis court at our disposal and we had some very good games in idyllic and most unwarlike surroundings. The routine flying and training continued and the 'phoney' war went on for RNAS Eastleigh until late October 1939 when a signal arrived from the Admiralty instructing Captain R T Partridge RM to join 803 Squadron which was equipped with Skuas and stationed at Wick. For me the 'phoney' war was coming to an end.

Wick. Where the hell was it? I got hold of an AA book and to my dismay and astonishment discovered that if you went up the east coast of England and Scotland almost as far north as you could you would arrive there, just 17 miles south of John-o-Groats! My instructions were to proceed by rail as soon as possible and my 'soonest as possible' reaction was to visit the station commander to persuade him that to turn over the duties of Passive Defence Officer would need at least two or three days. He saw through my subterfuge instantly, and with a smile said, 'You can have a forenoon to turn over your PD duties followed by 48 hours leave for goodbyes.' That afternoon I managed to get a lift in a Fairey Swordfish to RNAS Ford which was close to my home at Worthing and even closer to my girlfriend at Rustington. I had my leave, said my farewells and then was driven back by my girl to Eastleigh on a dreadful, windy, rainy day. It was a sad journey; we didn't know when or where we'd ever meet again and trying to be cheerful and normal was difficult. I later had a letter from her saying that her return drive alone, with rain outside and tears inside, was very, very painful.

With all goodbyes over I now drew a first-class (thank God) railway warrant from Eastleigh to Wick, and off I went. The journey was boring but uneventful, the single line from Inverness to Wick taking almost as long as the whole of the previous part of the trip. I arrived at Wick station in the evening after dark and was very relieved to find that 803 Squadron had arranged transport for me and my baggage to the hotel which had been requisitioned as an Officers Mess. I have happy memories of this little hotel and can remember to this day those magnificent

Scottish teas we used to sit down to in the evening. I also remember the very glamorous young receptionist who wore an engagement ring and made it more than clear that no Naval or Marine officer was of the least interest to her.

I don't want to be unkind about Wick as I am sure it is dear to many a resident and visitor: but I was there for just one month, the month of November 1939, and it seemed a very grey and forbidding place. Fortunately we had a great deal to do and I flew every day except one, clocking up over 60 hours which was a lot for a fighter pilot at that time. The flying consisted almost entirely of 100 mile patrols out to sea and back to give cover to any merchant shipping being attacked by enemy aircraft. When the weather allowed we patrolled at 10,000-12,000 feet and when the weather was bad almost at sea level. It was hard and rather boring work and during the whole month I never saw anything. On odd occasions others of the squadron did now and again surprise an enemy aircraft attacking a merchant ship and if they didn't shoot them down they certainly frightened them off.

One day, however, 25th November, was different. A signal came through to say that major units of the fleet were being shadowed by enemy aircraft north-east of the Shetland Isles and 803 Squadron's commander decided to take four Skuas up there to deal with the situation. I was one of the four and we took off at about 1300 in very squally, poor weather. We eventually found the ships about three hours later, only to be told to return to base immediately as enemy aircraft had departed. The weather was deteriorating and darkness not far off so 803 leader decided to land and spend the night at Sumburgh in the Shetlands where there was a small (very small!) aerodrome and a Royal Air Force detachment. We all managed to land safely and refuelled, spent the night there and returned to Wick early the next morning. I think it may be interesting to realize that at the time of which I am writing there were only about 15 Royal Marine officers flying with the Fleet Air Arm and yet in 803 Squadron where I was Red sub-section leader my number 2 and number 3 were both Royal Marines. Of course without fail we were dubbed 'The Thin Red Line'.

My last flight from Wick is recorded in my Log Book as taking off at 0850 on 30th November for a flight of 2 hrs 40 mins at 15,000 feet on fighter patrol. It was my last because on 1st December a signal came from the Admiralty instructing me to form 804 Squadron at RNAS Hatston in the Orkneys. I was not to be the Commanding Officer of the squadron but second in command, the CO designate not being available at the moment. So here I was once again heading even further north and further away from my roots and loves in Sussex. But this time not by train, all my belongings were crammed into the back seat of a Swordfish and off we headed, to land at Royal Naval Air Station Hatston, a mile or two outside Kirkwall, on the main island. Here once again, the Mess was in a small hotel the Navy had taken over; I found it most comfortable with good food and really, in a way, too civilized for the other side of our lives, the operational flying. I loved the rugged, wild, wind-swept grandeur of the Orkneys, and promised myself a re-visit in more peaceful times — regrettably a promise yet to be kept. As the hotel was some distance from the airfield I bought myself a bicycle, primarily to get to and fro, but on my rare days off I used to ride out with some sandwiches and a bottle of beer and relax in remote and isolated splendour and beauty. Unfortunately this didn't happen often;

An evocative study of a Gloster Gladiator II in flight.

and perhaps it was just as well, as such pastimes didn't tend to foster my fighting spirit and determination to do or die.

After the war I was told that the Prime Minister, Winston Churchill, had decided that Scapa Flow had insufficient fighter protection and that a Fleet Air Arm fighter squadron was to be formed there immediately — and when he said immediately it really meant just that. It was to carry out this order that 804 Squadron was being formed in such a hurry. The aircraft and the pilots were coming in and after a few days I was able to tell the station commander that I had six aircraft operational and that soon the squadron would be completed. There was no accommodation for the ground crews at the field and they were housed in large buildings, such as the Town Hall, in Kirkwall. I visited them from time to time to do what I could for their well-being and to encourage them. They were a fine, cheerful, loyal and willing lot, sleeping in pretty spartan conditions, mostly on the floor.

Now and again the odd German aircraft or two used to appear, usually Heinkel He 111s, at great height, probably on reconnaissance, but occasionally a stick of bombs was dropped near the aerodrome and the enemy were then chased off by us. I should have mentioned before that 804 was equipped with single-seater Gloster Gladiators, the last of the biplane fighters (and not to be sneezed at). I am not claiming that they were in the Spitfire or Hurricane class but they were rugged, easy to fly and very manoeuverable. They had an excellent rate of climb and I can remember that one day when I had to chase after a reported Peacock (unidentified aircraft) to 30,000 feet when visibility was maximum I could see the Orkneys and Shetlands, Fair Isle and practically the whole of Scotland. Unfortunately the only thing I didn't see was the Peacock.

With the squadron acting in this fighter role we obviously had to have at least some aircraft at immediate readiness, and I found that with the pilots accommodated in a hotel a mile or more from their aircraft the delay between an alarm and getting to those aircraft was unacceptable. There was a large, long hut on the airfield used for storage and I managed to convince the station CO that this must be converted into living quarters and Mess for the aircrews of 804 Squadron. This was very successful as we now lived 'on the job' and really were available. Of course, we sacrificed some comfort, sleeping in dormitories and eating issue rations, but nobody minded and it did a lot to build the squadron into a really close team.

Our usual routine was one sub-flight of three at immediate readiness, one at readiness and one at stand-by. The fourth was off duty unless it was known that something special was expected. When no aircaft were airborne on patrol we always had one machine manned and warmed up at the end of the duty runway ready for instant take-off. One day I was on the end-of-the-runway duty and it so happened

A naval Gloster Gladiator at HMS *Sparrowhawk* (RNAS Hatston) about 1940. The Sea Gladiator was a stopgap measure to give the Fleet Air Arm a 'modern' fighter to operate from carriers until the arrival of the Skua and Fairey Fulmar. It saw action off Norway from HMS *Glorious* and in the Mediterranean aboard HMS *Eagle*.

that on either side of the end of this particular runway was a very large dump of boxed bombs and ammunition. As I sat there in my cockpit ready for take-off I noted an armourer moving among the stores, probably checking and counting. I also noticed that the wind had changed and that this runway was now well across wind. I called up on my R/T and asked permission to take up position at the end of a runway now into wind and this was granted. I had only just settled down in my new position when there was a really shattering explosion from the ammunition dump at the end of the runway I had just left — the whole lot had gone up! Tragically all that was found of the armourer was a small piece of what the doctor decided was spine, and absolutely nothing else. Truly it's an 'ill-wind'.

Two days later I was starting to taxi my Gladiator down the runway in order to take up my readiness position into wind at the far end when a high flying He 111 dropped a stick of bombs just off the side of the airfield. I was frightened out of my wits and not knowing whether another stick was about to drop across the airfield, and me, I slammed the throttle open and took off downwind. I, of course, never caught up with the Heinkel but was later congratulated by the station CO for my presence of mind and for getting airborne so quickly.

About the middle of December I began to feel a bit off-colour and after sticking it out for two days I had to report sick. The diagnosis was tonsillitis and so it was to bed feeling very, very ill. There was talk of moving me to the hospital ship in Scapa Flow, but transport difficulties and my poor state prevented this. I recovered after about a week and was ordered to take 10 days leave to convalesce. So it happened that my first Christmas of the war was spent at home in Sussex, but it was to be the last for some years to come.

After Christmas I returned to Hatston, first by train to Inverness and then by de Havilland Dominie of Scottish Airways. These Dominie trips always used to amuse me because if the pilot had a full load of passengers, about seven or eight I think, he used to taxi out to the end of the duty runway and when in position for take-off he would turn around and casually ask the rear four passengers to come forward and kneel in the passageway just behind him so that it would be easier for him to get the aircraft tail up when taking off. Of course, as soon as airborne, the four passsengers returned to their seats.

On rejoining the squadron I found that the proper Commanding Officer had arrived, so I was now second in command and not a little relieved to hand over the work and responsibility of command. January, February and March of 1940 were spent on routine local defensive flying, mostly investigating radar reports of incoming unidentified aircraft, although I do see an entry in my Log Book for 16th March which records 'enemy attack on Scapa Flow and Orkneys at 1950 hours'. The whole squadron got airborne but in the gathering darkness no contacts were made and we all had a hell of a job landing back at the airfield as there were no flares or runway lighting. But it was very exciting and, as far as I can remember, no damage was caused either to the Fleet in Scapa or to us.

It was 1st April 1940, the first April Fool's Day of the war, when a signal arrived from the Admiralty saying: 'Captain R T Partridge RM appointed Commanding Officer of 800 Squadron immediately'. Things move fast in wartime and, if you last, promotion can be quick!

HMS *Ark Royal* wearing Spanish Civil War neutrality markings on the forward 4.5 inch gun turret early in 1939. The third ship to carry the name, and most famous of them all, it entered service in 1938 and was finally sunk, after many false alarms, on 13th November 1941. Ark Royal could carry up to 60 aircraft.

HMS *Ark Royal* had arrived at Scapa Flow and disembarked her two Skua squadrons, 800 and 803, to Hatston. So here I was back to Skuas again, but this time with a squadron of my own and the knowledge that immediately *Ark Royal* was ordered to sea we would be off to land on her and with her wherever she went. This move for me also meant leaving the accommodation I had improvised for 804 Squadron on the airfield and returning to the hotel. I missed the camaraderie of our old rough quarters but at the same time couldn't help enjoying the relative comforts of the hotel.

My squadron observer was Robin Bostock, a senior Lieutenant RN and perhaps a year or so younger than me. He was a quiet personality but immensely experienced and capable as a Fleet Air Arm observer. We got on very well together and I had complete faith in his professional ability; I like to think that he had the same faith in me as a pilot.

The other Skua squadron, 803, was commanded by an old friend of mine, Lieutenant William Lucy RN. We had been together on and off for many years, both at home and in the Far East and Mediterranean. In fact he was one of my tennis enthusiasts in the first days of the war at Eastleigh. He was a fine officer and pilot and as far as I could see completely fearless. Our two squadrons settled down to a steady routine of convoy patrols, investigating reported enemy attacks on merchant ships and similar tasks.

6

Sinking the Königsberg

On the not-too-frequent occasions when I could take a day off and hand over the running of my squadron to my senior pilot, I used to relax as best I could; sometimes by strolling round Kirkwall or gently exploring the surrounding countryside, anything in fact that was peaceful and in no way connected with flying and the war. But not so my friend Bill Lucy. As far as I could make out he spent all his off-duty time in the operations room, studying the reports coming in and hoping always that he would find some new target that he and his squadron could attack.

On one of my off days, (9th April 1940 to be exact) an excited Bill Lucy shattered my peace with a most outrageous plan. He told me that in the operations room he had seen a Royal Air Force reconnaissance report that said a German cruiser was lying alongside in Bergen harbour and, if I agreed, he proposed taking both squadrons across and dive-bombing her.

Though not a fire-eater like Bill I was certainly prepared to take reasonable risks for myself and my squadron, and obviously such an attack could not possibly be expected by the enemy and would therefore have that greatest advantage of all — surprise. But was this a reasonable risk?

I pointed out to Bill that Bergen was about two hours flying each way in still air for Skuas and that our official endurance was only 4 hrs 20 mins; to which he replied that we both knew that we could stretch this a bit and that if we didn't hang around over the target too long we should be able to make it. My next observation was that there were long-range German fighters, Me 110s, at Stavanger and that we would be sitting targets for them. Not, Bill said, if we carry out a surprise attack, straight in and out; they will not have time to get up from Stavanger and intercept us. I then asked him how the hell we carried out a surprise attack on a target that lay 30 to 40 miles up the Bergen Fjord; to which he replied that we should take off at night at a time that would allow us to arrive over Bergen at sunrise. Non-fire-eater Partridge then played his trump card by saying that though such a raid might just be possible the station CO would never authorize such a risky undertaking; but Bill's reply was that he had already discussed it with the CO and that if I agreed we had authorization to carry it out tomorrow. I must admit that on my own I don't think I would even have thought up this plan and all credit for its inception must go to Bill Lucy. His enthusiasm and confidence was however having an effect on me and I was beginning to think it might, with luck, be possible. After a little further discussion I agreed and we reported to the station CO who gave us the order to go ahead.

Bill and I didn't want to discuss our objective too widely for security reasons; the last thing we wanted was a reception committee waiting for us at Bergen. We decided that plans could be made just by ourselves and our two squadron observers, and the four of us retired to the operations room to work out how and what we were going to do. As I have said before my squadron observer was Robin Bostock, but Robin at this moment was on loan to Coastal Command, RAF. Many naval observers were on loan in this manner to the RAF, not because they were better navigators but because of their inbred skill at recognizing and identifying warships from the air. There was little chance of a RN officer who had lived with ships all his service life mistaking, say, a German pocket battleship for one of our City Class cruisers, and such instant and accurate identification could be vital. With Robin away I was given Lieutenant Commander Geoffrey Hare as my observer. He was senior to me and vastly experienced and I cannot speak too highly of the support he gave me or of the excellence of his navigation that brought me over the target at exactly the planned time.

Studying the maps and charts in the operations room we decided that there were few alternatives open to us and we settled on the following simple plan:

1. Briefing our aircrews to be at 0415.
2. Take off at 0500.
3. One 500 lb SAP (semi-armour-piercing) bomb, eight 20 lb bombs and full .303 ammunition to be carried by each aircraft.
4. Nine aircraft from 803 and seven from 800 to take part. (This was dictated by the availability of aircraft and aircrew).
5. Course to and from the target to be given to each pilot. (This was because observers were only carried in the squadron CO's aircraft. The backseat crew in the other aircaft were not trained in navigation but were telegraphist air gunners, trained in W/T communications and gunnery). Thus, if any aircraft got separated from the leader the pilot would at least have a course to steer.
6. Squadrons would form up over Hatston aerodrome and the crossing would be made at 10,000 feet in open formation.
7. Rendezvous after the attack would be the small island with lighthouse off the entrance to Bergen Fjord at 5000 feet. Leaders would wait no longer than five minutes for stragglers.
8. The course to be taken was the shortest one, direct from Hatston to Bergen. This course was dictated by the endurance of the Skua and pilots were warned not to do anything unnecessary that would waste fuel.

These were the outlines of the plan and detailed arrangements such as the order of take-off, order of attacking and queries from the aircrew would be explained at the briefing.

All that was left to do now was to warn the squadrons, aircrews and ground crews, that they were required for a fully armed operation taking off at 0500 and that the final aircrew briefing would be at 0415. Then it was just a question of waiting.

Waiting, as far as I was concerned, was the worst part of an operation of this sort. By 1515 in the afternoon I had visited the squadron, seen the armourers arming the aircraft, chatted to the other ground crews and to the aircrews, and there was nothing left for me but return to the hotel and try not to ponder too deeply on what lay ahead. I never found this an easy thing to do (I suppose everbody suffers from pre-operational nerves to a lesser or greater degree), and I always admired the bomber crews who carried out 30, 60 or more missions over Germany without cracking up. At least we were not called on to do this sort of thing with the regularity of those in Bomber Command.

I didn't have a very happy evening, making a poor effort at eating some tea and supper. I went to bed at 2100 and dozed fitfully until called with a cup of tea and sandwiches at 0330; and what a ghastly hour that is for a show of calmness, determination and leadership. However, as soon as I had something to do I felt better, and back at the airfield briefing my aircrews I didn't really have time for all those craven thoughts that plagued me at the hotel; just that nagging queasy feeling in the tummy remained, and an indecision as to whether one final visit to the loo would be advisable.

I watched my aircrews' faces when I told them what we were going to do. If their reactions were the same as mine originally were they didn't show it; they took it calmly and magnificently. There were a few questions and answers and then I warned the pilots to take extra care about the take-off and forming up in the dark. The Skua with full armament and fuel was not very nice or easy to fly; it tended to be unstable fore and aft and would remain so until some of the fuel had been used

A typical Blackburn Skua, this picture gives a good impression of the size of the aircraft.

up. I can only liken it to driving a car which tends to wander and needs constant steering even on a straight road. The last thing we wanted was a prang or two before we had even started.

Just before 0500 there was the muffled report of a Coffman starter. One engine sprang into life, closely followed by another, and another until all other sounds were drowned by the shattering noise of 16 Bristol Perseus engines running up. No time for nerves now; pilots were too busy checking their instruments and watching for their turn to taxi out for take-off. At 0500 Bill Lucy roared down the runway and got airborne, to be followed at intervals by the rest of his squadron. Then it was my turn. Followed by my pilots we gingerly flew round above the airfield in the dark as we gradually joined up in formation at 3000 feet. Then Bill swung round on a course for Bergen, climbing slowly to reach 10,000 feet. We levelled out at that height and settled down to our most economical speed of 140 knots. It was important that leaders should keep a constant speed and that followers should not drop astern; excessive use of throttle to catch up or slow down meant more fuel used, and we didn't have any of that to spare!

I settled down 200 feet above and a few hundred yards out on Bill Lucy's starboard quarter. For some reason I always preferred flying on the right when in formation, I don't know why. It was a dark night but there were stars which helped, and I had no difficulty in keeping the other squadron in view, unless we ran into cloud. More time, of course, to think now and I felt sorry for the back seat crews who had even less to do than the pilots; at least we had our instruments to check, our formation to keep and could curse at the aircraft which refused to stay trimmed fore and aft.

My observer called me up on the intercom and told me that he reckoned we had just passed the halfway mark and were well set to arrive on time. He also pointed out the whispy clouds that were beginning to form and said that he thought they might increase. I had already noticed them and told him that if I lost contact with the other squadron I would climb to 12,000 feet and he would have to navigate me to the target. He seemed very calm and happy about this.

The Bristol Perseus engine we were flying behind was the first of the sleeve-valve ones, and as such was as smooth as a sewing machine. Cruising along behind it had almost a soporific effect and, had the occasion not been so important, one's attention could easily have wandered after an hour or so at steady height and speed. The cloud was increasing: it was now almost three-tenths and occasionally I would lose sight of Bill Lucy's squadron. But on we went as smoothly as ever, both squadrons in fairly open formation. I was beginning to lose sight of them more often now and began to climb to 11,000 feet so that there would be a vertical separation between us. Suddenly I knew I had lost them and in the dark it was most unlikely I would pick them up again. I told Lieutenant Commander Hare, my observer, that I was out of contact with 803 Squadron, that I was climbing to 12,000 feet and would be carrying out an attack independent of the other squadron. This separation of the squadrons would mean that instead of the continuous surprise attack of 16 diving Skuas, one squadron or the other was probably going to attack after an interval, thus minimizing the effect of surprise and certainly alerting the defences. There was nothing to be done about it and we had discussed and recognized this possibility.

Faint signs of the approaching dawn were now showing and I could already make out details of my nearest aircraft. I looked at my watch; it was 0640 and we had already been airborne for 1 hr 40 mins. Ten minutes later my observer asked me to increase speed to 150 knots as he reckoned we had fallen a little behind schedule when climbing to 12,000 feet, and he also asked me to keep a lookout ahead for the Norwegian coastline. Fear, excitement, apprehension, anticipation, call it what you will, was beginning to rise now, with that familiar feeling in the pit of the stomach. Suddenly I saw it, the coast of Norway; Geoffrey Hare saw it too and said 'I think we are bang on, maintain this course and keep an eye open for our rendezvous island and lighthouse'. It was daylight now and shortly before 0655 we both spotted the island just off the Bergen Fjord fine on our port bow. I glanced around and below for the other squadron, hoping that I could rejoin, but although the cloud had cleared away as we approached the coast there was no sign of them. The sun was just beginning to rise in a bright golden ball above the mountains which we knew cradled Bergen down to the water-line.

Calm, precise instructions were now coming from the rear cockpit over the inter-com: 'Start losing height at 300 feet per minute, speed 200 knots and follow the fjord'. I eased forward on the stick, closed my following aircraft in a little, felt the speed building up, 170 knots, 190 knots, 200 knots, and held it at that. No time for any feelings now other than intense concentration that was making me sweat a little. Suddenly, ahead of us was Bergen, looking quiet and peaceful in the sparkling, early morning sunlight. To port were three large fuel storage tanks and ahead and to star-board ships, but merchant ships only — no cruiser. There was no sign of activity of any sort, no enemy fighters and no AA fire.

We were almost down to 8000 feet when we spotted her, a long, thin, grey shape lying alongside a jetty. I pulled away to port in order to make a great sweep up to the mountains and over the town of Bergen itself and so attack out of the rising sun.

Now I was heading back towards the German cruiser and concentrating hard to get my Skua and those following me into the correct position for starting our dive.

The attack on the Königsberg, monochrome painting by C E Turner   FAA Museum collection

This position was, in my opinion, of the utmost importance. Dive-bombing is a most accurate, perhaps the most accurate, method of delivering a bomb onto a selected target, and the angle of dive determines the accuracy of the attack: too steep and the dive tends to get even steeper and out of control; too shallow and the target tends to disappear under one and accuracy is lost. But start the dive in just the right position so that you are going down at 65°, then in a good dive-bomber like the Skua with its large flaps accurate bombing becomes almost easy.

Having reached a suitable position, I did a 90° turn to port, eased back on the stick, flaps down, further back on the stick, a half stall turn to starboard and then I was in a well-controlled dive with the cruiser held steady in my sights. I was losing height and down to 6000 feet with the target still held steady in my sights when to my astonishment ahead of me in the dive I saw a Skua release its bomb and go racing away at water level. I later found out that this was the last aircraft of 803 Squadron so, quite fortuitously, we were going to carry out our planned continuous raid with all 16 aircraft!

I was attacking the ship from bow to stern and the only resistance being offered was coming from a light Bofors type AA gun on the fo'c'sle which kept firing throughout the engagement; tracer bullets were gliding past on either side. My dive was still firm and controlled with the ship held steady in my sights and I could see water and oil gushing out of her below the waterline and guessed that she had already been damaged. Down to 3500 feet now and beginning to watch my height; mustn't lose accuracy by releasing too high and mustn't release too low and risk blowing myself up. 3000 feet, 2500, 2000, and at 1800 I pressed the release button on the stick and let my bombs go, turning violently away to starboard and then down to water level when well clear.

As we raced low down the fjord at full throttle Lieutenant Commander Hare was telling me that he reckoned we had had a near miss on the ship's starboard bow when he suddenly said 'MTB travelling fast ahead of us', and there was a motor torpedo boat, at full speed with decks crowded with servicemen. I turned towards her and as we got near gave a long burst with my front guns and saw men jumping off and into the water. We were being fired on now by AA batteries in the woods on the steep side of the fjord and in this mad dash we were making I was tempted to have a go at them too. Sensibly, I resisted this rash impulse and continued to climb to 5000 feet over our rendezvous. There I saw the glad sight of Bill Lucy with all his squadron but one, and I was soon joined by mine. Circling, waiting for Bill's straggler, was bad for my nerves as the excitement of the attack and getaway began to wear off. As I sat there jittery in my cockpit imagining hordes of Me110s arriving at any moment I was vastly relieved to see a single-engined monoplane approaching; Bill's missing Skua. We learnt later that this aircraft had dived with 803 Squadron but had had a hang-up and couldn't release its bombs. The pilot, determined not to jettison them, had laboriously climbed back to 8000 feet, circled over Bergen again, and carried out a lone attack after we had all gone. This time the AA gun on the fo'c'sle was no longer firing.

Sixteen aircraft into the attack and sixteen out! It seemed too good to be true: and we had certainly damaged that ship, perhaps we had even sunk her. We were now on course for home and had been airborne for some two and a half hours with the best part of another two hours flying ahead of us. It would be touch and go, and should a head wind get up it seemed extremely likely that some of us at least would get very wet feet. After ten minutes on our homeward course — disaster! The outer aircraft on my starboard side suddenly went into a vertical dive and hit the sea under full power; all that remained was a large circle of disturbed water and a few pieces of wreckage. There was nothing that could possibly be done save to continue on our long flight home. It was never possible to discover what had happened but it seemed likely that either the aircraft had been hit and succumbed to elevator control failure or the pilot had been wounded, held out so far, and then suddenly collapsed.

There was seven-tenths cloud now and moderate visibility as we steadily flew on at our most economical speed. By 0900 I had been airborne for 3 hrs 45 mins, which meant 35 minutes of our official endurance left, but still no sight of ship or land. I was now frequently looking at my watch and anxiously watching my fuel gauges, and I am sure everybody else was doing the same. It would be ironic if we all ended up in the drink, after such a successful attack. The time was now 0935 and I had been airborne for our official endurance of 4 hrs and 20 mins when to my utmost relief my observer said quietly over the intercom: 'Stronsay fine on our starboard bow'. Stronsay was the most easterly of the Orkney Islands and we were almost home.

I landed at 0945 having been in the air for four and a half hours. Some of the aircraft clocked up five minutes longer, depending on the order in which they had taken off and landed. Some marvellous stories ran round the squadron for days afterwards among the ground crews — 'He didn't have enough petrol in his tanks to cover a penny'; 'As he taxied in towards me his engine cut dead, his tanks were completely dry'; 'His engine cut out as he touched down' — a certain amount of exaggeration no doubt, but it was assuredly true that we had mighty little to spare.

There was great excitement, congratulations and euphoria whilst we were being debriefed before going off to breakfast. General opinion among the naval pilots and observers was that our target had been a Köln class cruiser and we were all certain that she had been badly damaged, perhaps even sunk. This was confirmed later by a report from RAF reconnaissance flights and photographs which showed that the ship was sunk alongside the jetty. Later, intelligence from Norway established that she was in fact the cruiser *Königsberg*. Bill Lucy's rash, mad plan had worked and for the loss of only one aircraft, which seemed a small price to pay; and so I suppose it was except to those directly connected: sorrowing mums and dads, brothers and sisters, fiancées perhaps and girl friends. They had received a blow that for some might last a lifetime but which we, distressed as we were at the loss of good friends, had to put as soon as possible from our minds, or accept as the fortunes of war in the full knowledge that it might be anybody's turn next. Grieving over losses is bad for morale and efficiency and from now on our losses were to mount rapidly: it was not long before the only surviving officer of my squadron was myself.

The sinking of the *Königsberg* was a historic event, demonstrating for the first time the effectiveness of the dive-bomber against major warships. This was a lesson that was not lost upon the Japanese and American Navies as was demonstrated time after time in those terrific battles that were to take place later in the war of the

The cruiser *Königsberg,* launched in March 1929, was 570 feet long, displaced 6000 tons, carried a crew of 571 and could steam at 32 knots. Armed with nine 5.9 inch guns in three triple turrets and 14 anti-aircraft guns, *Königsberg* was an important element of the German fleet. The layout of the main armament was unusual in that two of the three turrets were mounted aft.

It is interesting to note that the first victims of British Naval air action in both world wars were German cruisers of the same name. During 1915 aircraft of the RNAS spotted for Naval gunfire that destroyed SMS *Königsberg* in the Rufiji Delta, German East Africa.

These photographs, including one frame from a cine film, were taken by Norwegians immediately after the Skua raid. They show *Königsberg* on fire at the quayside where she went down by the head, capsized and sank.

Pacific. Inexplicably, this lesson was ignored by our Admiralty, or as a well-known author on naval affairs so succinctly put it to me, was greeted with 'roars of indifference', and it was not long before the Skua was phased out of operational flying because of its poor performance as a fighter. A poor fighter it may have been but in my opinion it was a great dive-bomber and used properly in surprise attacks or with adequate fighter cover it could have played a more significant role in the early war years. As it was the Blackburn Skua had its finest hour in the attack on the *Königsberg* and so has its place in naval aviation history.

Lieutenant W Lucy RN and I were awarded the DSO for this attack and our two observers the DSC. Poor Bill was not to learn of his award for a short time later he was shot down and killed while attacking a Heinkel. I had lost a very great friend and the Fleet Air Arm a very fine officer and pilot.

I quote below the citation in the *London Gazette* dated Tuesday, 7th May, 1940 that Bill was never to see.

> 'The King has been graciously pleased to give orders for the following appointments to the Distinguished Service Order for daring and resource in the conduct of hazardous and successful operations by the Fleet Air Arm against the enemy, especially on the coast of Norway:-
> Captain Richard Thomas Partridge, Royal Marines
> Lieutenant William Paulet Lucy, Royal Navy.'

SUPPLEMENT

TO

The London Gazette

Of TUESDAY, the 7th of MAY, 1940

Published by Authority

Registered as a newspaper

THURSDAY, 9 MAY, 1940

Admiralty, Whitehall.
9th May, 1940.

The KING has been graciously pleased to give orders for the following appointments to the Distinguished Service Order for daring and resource in the conduct of hazardous and successful operations by the Fleet Air Arm against the enemy, especially on the coast of Norway:—

To be Companions of the Distinguished Service Order:

Captain Richard Thomas Partridge, Royal Marines.
Lieutenant William Paulet Lucy, Royal Navy.

His Majesty has also been graciously pleased to approve the following awards for similar services:—

The Distinguished Service Cross:

Lieutenant-Commander Geoffrey Hare, Royal Navy.
Lieutenant Harry Ernest Richard Torin, Royal Navy.
Lieutenant Michael Charles Edward Hanson, Royal Navy.
Acting Lieutenant Edward Winchester Tollemache Taylour, Royal Navy.
Midshipman (A) Thomas Anthony McKee.

The Distinguished Service Cross (Bar):

Acting Lieutenant Edward Winchester Tollemache Taylour, Royal Navy.

The Distinguished Service Medal:

Petty Officer Airman Harold Arthur Monk, FX.76290.
Acting Petty Officer Airman Howard Gresley Cunningham, FX.76292.

Mentions in Despatches:

Lieutenant-Commander Aubrey St. John Edwards, Royal Navy.
Lieutenant William Paulet Lucy, Royal Navy.
Lieutenant Michael Charles Edward Hanson, Royal Navy.
Lieutenant Robert Southey Bostock, Royal Navy.
Lieutenant Cecil Howard Filmer, Royal Navy.
Lieutenant Kenneth Vyvyan Vincent Spurway, Royal Navy.
Acting Lieutenant Edward Winchester Tollemache Taylour, Royal Navy.
Acting Petty Officer Airman Howard Gresley Cunningham, FX.76292.
Petty Officer Airman Christopher James Edwin Cotterill, F.55040.
Naval Airman First Class Frederick Percival Dooley, FX.79189.
Leading Airman Maurice Hall, FX.76325.

Arado Ar196A-3 of 4/Bordfliegergruppe 196 (T3 + HH) salvaged from the sunken *Königsberg* which could carry two of these catapult launched floatplanes. The building in the background displays evidence of damage from the earlier raid.

Königsberg during salvage operations in 1944.

7

Final days at Hatston

Operation Bergen was just one day in our routine at Hatston and within two hours of landing back the ground crews had re-fuelled, re-armed and serviced the aircraft and we were once again operationally available. To my relief there was no further call on our services that day, but the next day I was in the air again at 1030 for a three hour convoy patrol and again at 1845 for a similar patrol. It was hard and tiring work, but worse was to come.

The station CO sent for me and said it had been decided that single Skuas should be sent over to Bergen on what were called offensive reconnaissance flights and asked my opinion. I couldn't admit that the idea scared the pants off me, which it did, but said that I did not think such flights were justified unless there was a definite and important target to be attacked, in which case more than one aircraft would be needed. My diplomatically couched advice went unheeded but I think the CO was under pressure from the Admiralty, and I carried out four of those dicey missions on 12th, 14th, 17th and 20th April 1940.

On the first two my official instructions were to carry out reconnaissance, dive bombing and front gun attacks on enemy shipping; if no target was found I was to jettison bombs and return to base. On both occasions we flogged all the way across the North Sea and spent 15 minutes of valuable flying time surveying Bergen harbour from 14,000 feet. As far as I could see there were no military targets. There were several merchant ships, nationality unknown, and they could be and probably were neutral; then there were the big oil storage tanks which always tempted me as a target, but they were presumably operated and maintained by Norwegian civilians, and although I asked several times, i never did get clear orders to regard them as a legitimate target. It must be remembered that in those early days of the war indiscriminate and unrestricted bombing had not yet started. So on these first two trips, each of four and a half hours, we found no target, jettisoned our bombs and returned safely, tired and frustrated.

For the third trip my orders were the same, and my observer and I thought the results would also be the same. Well they were, in so much as we found no target and once again jettisoned our bombs; but the weather was windy and when we had left Hatston we were flying with a strong wind on our starboard beam. When we started our return flight my observer said that he didn't like the look of the sea. I

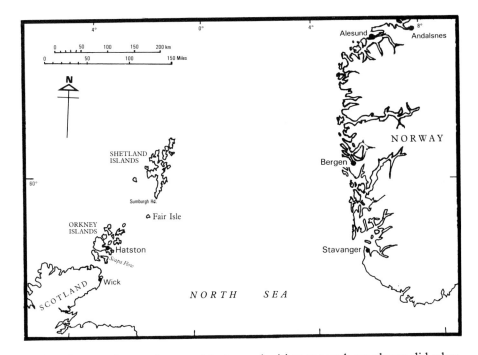

took a glance and to me it seemed just as uninviting as rough sea always did when you were faced with a two hour flight in a single-engined aircraft. But that wasn't what he meant; he had noticed that the wind-whipped white crests of the waves were now in a different direction and he reckoned that the gale had increased a lot and veered 90° so that we now had a strong head wind to contend with. We had spent 20 minutes over Bergen and it seemed probable that we might not have enough fuel to get us back to Hatston. Now, if you look at a map you will see that the Shetland Isles are some 70 to 80 miles closer to Bergen than the Orkneys and the RAF airfield at Sumburgh at the southern tip of the Shetlands was officially our diversion airfield in emergency. The situation we were in was an emergency and showed only too clearly how little there was to spare for the Skua in these long trips across the North Sea. So I asked my observer to give me a course for Sumburgh. When we arrived there we had been airborne for 4 hrs 35 mins and I wasted no time in preparing for a landing, only to be greeted on my final approach by a red Very light. This of course meant 'don't land'; but there was nowhere else and I couldn't circle Sumburgh waiting for an affirmative. I instantly decided to ignore the red and continued my landing; we touched down very nicely on the small grass airfield, ran 50 or 60 yards and then violently nosed up, tearing the whole engine out of its mountings and leaving it behind us. We continued for another 100 yards or so in this uncomfortable and undignified position until we juddered to a halt. No fire, no injuries and no engine! We were lucky to get away with it but really had had no option. The RAF, as usual, were very nice to us and very hospitable and told me that the airfield was waterlogged and unserviceable. Had I known this I would probably have made an emergency wheels-up landing, thereby much reducing the chances of a serious crash. We had come down at Sumburgh at 1315 after 4 hrs 35 mins in the air, and that afternoon a Swordfish arrived from Hatston and ferried us back to the Orkneys. On return I lodged a very strong protest about Hatston not knowing that their diversionary airfield was out of action.

Two days later I picked up a new Skua, number L2940, and this one, after many adventures, is now the only Blackburn Skua left in the world and is in the Fleet Air Arm Museum at Royal Naval Air Station Yeovilton. But more of that later.

My log book for the 20th April reads: 1040 Air Test of 25 minutes for new Skua L2940; and at 1440 I took off in her on my fourth and final lone trip to Norway. This time my orders were to attack enemy warships at Larvik, which was a port lying south-south-west from Oslo and some 80 miles further from the Orkneys even than Bergen. In addition the shortest route led directly over Stavanger which we believed was a German fighter base. As far as I was concerned this was certainly going to be a quick in and out raid with no hanging about looking for targets.

We crossed the North Sea at 12,000 feet, with weather good and visibility maximum, and we made a slight detour to take us about 20 miles south of Stavanger. As far as was known the Germans had no radar and there seemed a good chance that a lone aircraft would go undetected. We reached Larvik unmolested and after two circuits over the port it was very evident that there was little or no shipping there and certainly no target for us. So I said to myself 'Let's get the hell out of here' whilst we had the chance. My observer, Robin, and I had agreed to vary our return route so that it took us 20 miles to the north-east of Stavanger whereas we had been 20 miles south-west on our arrival flight. As I swung round on to the return course we were passing over the fjord leading up to Skien when Robin spotted an MTB at high speed. I was going to have to jettison my bombs somewhere but here at least was something that could be described as a military target and, quelling my qualms at dropping a 500lb semi armour piercing bomb on so small a target (it didn't seem fair somehow), I went into an attacking dive. The MTB took vigorous evasive action and was quite difficult to keep in my sights. It had one light AA gun which kept firing rather too accurately for my liking. I released my bombs at 2000 feet and the boat must have spotted this as it went into a violent and magnificent turn to port with the result that I missed by 50 to 100 yards on the starboard quarter. I must admit I had a sneaking feeling of relief that I hadn't blown it to pieces.

We continued on our pre-arranged course for Hatston and were passing over the great fjords south of Bergen when we spotted a real target, but now sadly we had no bombs. This was a submarine on the surface heading for Bergen. All I had left were my front guns and I reckoned that if I could get a long burst in on her at reasonably close range at least some of my armour piercing bullets might penetrate her pressure hull and do some damage. As I neared her, losing height to 4000 feet, she fired a four star white Very light which I presumed was the German recognition signal for the day. I replied with a friendly waggle of my aircraft wings hoping this would keep her on the surface. It worked and enabled me to get into position to go into a really steep screaming dive, all guns blazing. No flaps down this time for a steady controlled dive, just speed to get at her before she crash-dived. I could see the splashes raised all round her by my hail of bullets but by the time I was down to 800 feet she had completed a quite remarkable crash-dive and disappeared. There was no way of knowing what damage, if any, I had inflicted but I am quite certain that the U-boat crew had had some very unpleasant moments and I often wondered how long she deemed it prudent to remain submerged. What a pity I had wasted my bombs on that confounded MTB. All I could do was to regain height and resume course for the Orkneys and home. The rest of our trip was uneventful and we landed back at Hatston after 4 hrs 30 mins in the air. It was my last trip of this sort and, with hindsight, as the Americans would say, I still maintain that they were pushing our luck a bit and not really worth the risk of aircraft and experienced aircrews.

It was my last trip because next day orders came through for 800 and 803 Squadrons to stand by to embark in HMS *Ark Royal,* and I guessed rightly that once again I was going to find myself heading even further north.

German *Schnellboot* (E-boat) S19. One of five similar craft based in Bergen shortly after the invasion began.

To sea in HMS Ark Royal

We had two days to prepare and spent much of this time doing ADDLs (Aerodrome Dummy Deck Landings). Several of my newer pilots had never deck-landed a Skua and it was important that they got used to landing in the nose-up, controlled sinking attitude required for deck landing. It so happened that I had never deck landed a Skua either, but I kept that fact to myself as I thought it might be bad for morale! Actually I was not very worried about it because of certain characteristics of the Skua. I had been used to landing-on in Hawker Nimrods for several years past and this aircraft was powered by a Rolls Royce Kestrel which stretched a long way out in front of the pilot so that when the aircraft nose was up on the final approach its long and beautiful engine tended almost to obscure the view of the deck; and it was this lack of view which had always caused me the most difficulty. The Skua,

HMS *Ark Royal*

About to take the wire, Skua 6M lands back on HMS *Ark Royal*.

however, was very different. Here there was a short Bristol Perseus radial engine in front and the pilot sat very much higher in the cockpit; hence the view of the deck was almost unhindered. My squadron took off at 0520 and after a flight of 40 minutes I had landed-on with no trouble at all. I had come down first with instructions to report to the flying control position on the bridge so that I could advise the commander (flying), who was in charge of all flying to and from the carrier, as to the experience and capabilities of the squadron aircraft following. I advised that the pilots with no previous deck landing experience in Skuas should land last, thus reducing the chance of obstructing the flying deck by a crash. It turned out that everyone came on without difficulty first time which speaks highly for the Skua as a deck landing aircraft and for the pilots.

A word or two about my feelings for life in a carrier in wartime would not be out of place here. In peace I had always enjoyed carrier life at sea, especially in the Mediterranean and the Far East. The chief complaint in those days was that we did not always get enough flying. Now we were at war things were different, however, flying alternated between being too intense or too intermittent, and it was the latter I found most trying. Not unnaturally my action station was flying, but when 'Action Stations' was sounded it could quite often happen that my squadron, or perhaps just I myself, was not required. On such occasions I found everybody rushing at full speed to their appointed task and I had nothing to do — no flying, no job. My cabin was down in the bowels of the ship and was inboard with no

Bombing up Skua 6H of 800 Squadron. Note that even at this period RAF personnel were still aboard.

porthole. When Action Stations sounded I could hear all watertight doors being clanged shut and I felt trapped below decks, so I used to go up to the operations room. This was high up in the island superstructure and even there, with nothing to do, I would feel frightened and exposed whilst everybody else appeared so busy they didn't even seem to be aware that the ship was being bombed. I never got used to that and always envied those who were kept really hard at it when the carrier was under attack.

Ark Royal proceeded north until she was 150 miles off the coast midway up Norway and orders were that the Skua squadrons were to carry out offensive patrols against German bombers and, where possible, in support of Norwegian and our own troops. On the 25th April I was on a patrol with two other of my aircraft in the Namsos area lasting 4 hrs 20 mins, and next day a similar one of about two hours in the Andalsnes area. Both patrols were uneventful except that in the latter I flew over the beautiful little town of Molde, built almost entirely of traditional Norwegian timber, and was so sad to see that it was in flames from end to end. The Germans had virtually complete mastery in the air and could bomb defenceless little towns at leisure.

The next day, 27th April, orders called for a sub-flight of three Skuas, led by myself, to patrol again in the Andalsnes area. Another tiring routine job, I thought, and was very sceptical about seeing or doing anything useful. Little did I think that it would be several days before I returned to the ship and that then it was not to be by air!

At 1200 hours three Skuas of my squadron were ranged up on the flight deck ready for take-off and at 1235 we were airborne and heading for the Norwegian coast once again. After 50 minutes we crossed the coast at 11,000 feet near Molde. We were flying in very open formation so that my accompanying aircraft and crew could keep a good look-out and only have to glance at me as leader occasionally. Just after crossing the coast I spotted heavy artillery bursts in the sky ahead. I closed my accompanying aircraft in a little and headed at full speed towards these bursts. As we got closer I saw a Heinkel He 111 carrying out a bombing run on the sloop HMS *Flamingo*, which was lying fairly close in just off Andalsnes. The Heinkel was 1000 feet higher than we were and I was now climbing flat out to try to get above him, but before we could get anywhere near he dropped his bombs which missed and was away to the south with a good two miles lead.

Now the chase was on! I have spoken before about the poor performance of the Skua as a fighter and I guess our speed advantage over the German bomber was only 10 to 15 knots. After 10 minutes with throttles jammed wide open I was at the same height as my quarry and gaining slowly but surely on him. 600 yards astern of him now and his rear gunner started firing at me, though I was hardly within his range for accurate shooting, but the thought did cross my mind that he might have a lucky shot! Being the leader of my flight I was obviously going to arrive ahead of my other two aircraft who were also flat out and trying to keep up with me. I held my fire until I was about 400 yards astern when I opened up with a long burst, closed in to 300 yards and let him have the rest of 600 rounds per gun. I was now out of ammunition but the Heinkel had smoke pouring from his port engine and was being attacked from below by one of my other Skuas. He was also losing speed and there was no fire coming from his rear gunner. My observer asked me to pull out on the beam of the enemy so that he could have a go with his rear gun, and I started to do this, then decided against it. The Heinkel was losing height rapidly so further attack was unnecessary and seemed to me too much like kicking a man when he was down. I was later told not to be so chivalrous and that I should have blown him out of the sky: I'm still glad I didn't. Instead I called my other two aircraft off and when they had formed up on me asked my observer for a course back to the ship. There wasn't much time left for us to continue the patrol and I was of no use without front gun ammunition. Then suddenly, as I was swinging round onto our new course, my engine cut dead without warning and we were surrounded by a shattering silence ...

I had often thought about what I would do if I found myself in a really desperate situation. Sometimes I imagined I would panic, or perhaps even die of fright; but now that it had happened, to my astonishment I was in a mood of fatalistic calm with no panic whatsoever. I was to experience this same reaction on later occasions, but I think it would have been more creditable if my 'calm' had been more aggressive and less fatalistic. Outwardly, however, I appeared to be completely in control and unperturbed.

Our long chase lasting about 26 minutes had taken us inland in a southerly direction and certainly well out of gliding distance of the sea where there would have been a reasonable chance of a wheels-up crash landing and getting away with it. We were down to 11,000 feet now and gliding ever so silently, too silently! Below and around us there was nothing to be seen but snow and mountains, the most inhospitable and impossible terrain for a forced landing, and also impossible for baling out. Not much use to land by parachute on top of a snow-covered mountain and be subsequently frozen to death.

Still gliding at a steady 90 knots and now at 9000 feet, I asked Robin to keep a look-out on our port side for any possible landing place and I watched to starboard. My other two aircraft were circling round us under power and no doubt wondering what the hell I was up to. I had just warned Robin to buckle on his parachute in case we had to bale out when he shouted excitedly that there was a road on our port side. I looked to my left and sure enough there was a thin narrow road, dark against the surrounding snow, and leading up to several little buildings. More importantly, this road ran alongside the wide, open, level expanse of what must have been a frozen lake. We were down to 4000 feet and now I knew exactly what I had to do. Because of the mountains I could only approach for my wheels-up landing from one direction regardless of whether it was upwind, downwind or crosswind; in any case we didn't know which way the wind was blowing. At 3000 feet I was swinging round on to my final approach and flipped the lever down to lower my flaps for landing. Nothing happened — no engine, — no power for lowering flaps. Frantically I started pumping on the auxiliary hand pump which provided power for operating flaps and undercarriage in emergency. I had never used this before and was still pumping with one hand and flying with the other when we were down to 500 feet on our final approach. I got the flaps down shortly before beginning to level out for the actual landing. I had never landed wheels-up before but was trying to make a three pointer with tail slightly down to prevent the nose of the aircraft digging into the snow. Down to 20 feet, speed just about right, and easing back on the control column, holding her there, back on the control column a little more and we touched gently and slid smoothly on the snow for a hundred yards to rest with no damage to the aircraft other than the unavoidable bent tips of the propeller as it touched the ground. We were down, safe and alive. So far so good!

I flung off my fighting harness and roared at Robin to get out quickly in case of fire. Simultaneously we jumped from the aircraft and immediately sank waist deep into snow. Laboriously we floundered and sank through the snow until we were some 50 yards from the Skua. We turned and surveyed her lying there on her belly, our means of transport, our means of returning to the ship, our completely and utterly immobilised 'home'. My other two aircraft came roaring low over us and we gave them a thumbs up and a wave to which they replied with a friendly waggle of their wings, climbed away and headed off into the distance on a course back to *Ark Royal*. The silence now really was complete and we felt very, very alone.

We didn't know where we were so didn't know whether we were in Norwegian or German-held territory. In the aircraft there was a very secret piece of equipment connected with radar, and some code books used for W/T communications. It was essential that these should not fall into enemy hands, so as soon as we were certain the aircraft was not going to burst into flames we decided that we must destroy them. But how? The Skua was an all-metal aircraft and when you were standing alongside it on the ground seemed very large, and very solid. There was no hope of lighting a match and holding it under, say, a wing or tailplane and expecting it to catch fire. No, the answer was petrol and there was plenty of that left in the two main tanks and the smaller third one. These two main tanks were situated between the pilot's and observer's cockpits, and very easily accessible. It so happened that one of the few items of emergency equipment in the aircraft was a small axe, and of course we carried a Very pistol and cartridges for visual signalling. I decided therefore to put the axe through one of the main tanks and ignite the resulting flow of petrol by firing a Very light at it from a safe distance. We collected what gear we thought could be of any use to us, including Robin's binoculars, and I then swung the axe and with no difficulty at all made a great gash near the bottom of one of the main tanks and the petrol came gushing out. I jumped down with the Very pistol and four cartridges and struggled through the snow until I was about 20-30 yards behind the tail of the aircraft. I chose a red coloured cartridge as being appropriate for the job in hand, loaded the pistol and fired. The lovely red orb of light shot away towards the machine and landed in the rear cockpit just abaft the petrol tanks. There was a moment's pause and then a great roar as the petrol ignited. There was however something that I had forgotten — the 600 rounds of .303 ammunition for my observer's rear gun! As the heat intensified this started to go off and we were much too close for safety. We both floundered frantically through the snow amidst a fusillade of bullets until we were reasonably out of range.

There was nothing more to be done with our Skua now: the whole of the cockpit section and its secrets had been burnt out and it lay there a quietly smoking semi-ruin. Our one and only link with *Ark Royal* was broken, so we collected our few belongings and started struggling towards the road. Sometimes for a short distance the crust on top of the snow would hold us, and then more often it would give way

A Norwegian ski-patrol examines the wreck of the author's Skua on Lake Breidal

and we would be up to our waists cursing and swearing. The road was only about 400 yards away but it took us a good half hour to get there, only to be met with a quite unexpected setback. The road itself was an unmade dirt road which lay under five feet of snow. What we had seen from the air was grit from the surface which had been drawn up or somehow risen to the top of the snow, appearing from a height of 5,000 feet to be a nice solid road we could walk on. Now it turned out that the snow on it was even softer than on the lake and it was quite unusable.

We had landed on the lake at 1410 and it was now after 1500. It was a lovely day with bright sunshine and quite warm, really too warm when struggling through the snow. We both knew however that at this time of the year some thousands of feet up in the Norwegian mountains the temperature would fall far below freezing after sunset. Somehow we had to find shelter before nightfall, and we knew that our only chance was to reach the huts we had spotted from the air at the end of the lake. I don't think the distance to them was more than one and a half to two miles and with skis or snow-shoes I guess we could have done it in half an hour. As it was it took us just over two hours of the most exhausting and frustrating struggle I can remember. We would walk a few paces on good hard snow, then down we would go waist deep again. We encouraged each other, swore at each other, pleaded with each other and even at times managed a laugh when one of us sank even deeper than usual. Soaked with sweat and exhausted we made it at about 1700 after a two-hour struggle.

There were three huts, or wooden cabins, about twice the size of a large garden shed, but they looked solid and weatherproof enough. The first was locked with its windows boarded up and we couldn't get in. The second looked more promising because even if the door was locked the windows were unboarded and it would be easy to break the glass. As it turned out we didn't even have to do that, as one of the windows was unlatched and we just climbed in and unlocked the door from the inside. We stood and surveyed our castle. There was no doubt that it was dirty, but for people in our condition it contained treasures that were quite beyond price — two wooden bunks with blankets (dirty!), a bench and table, a primus stove and paraffin, an iron stove and wood, two very old saucepans, the odd spoon and fork (very dirty!) and best of all a small sack of oatmeal. What more could two castaways want?

We spread the map we had salvaged from the aircraft on the table and pored over it, trying to decide where we were. I said jokingly to Robin, 'You're the navigator, where the hell are we? In Norwegian or German territory?' Poor old Robin grinned ruefully, and admitted that his navigation during the chase, whilst I was hammering away at the Heinkel with my front guns, had been nil. He drew a rough circle on the map and said that his best guess was that we were somewhere inside it and alongside a largish lake. The trouble was that his circle had a radius of about 15 miles and Norway is literally dotted with lakes big and small. We were lost!

We had taken off at 1230 which meant that from about 1130 we had been making preparations for the flight. We had both had a good breakfast at 0830 but no lunch. When you were about to embark on a four and a half hour flight in an aircraft like a Skua you had to be careful what you ate and drank during the hour or two before take-off. Anything that was going to encourage calls of nature had to be strictly avoided. For the pilot, at any rate, to answer such a call was practically impossible.

The result now was that we were both tired and hungry, very hungry. We had already decided that we must stay in the hut for the night and that if we could get a good rest and something to eat we would review our situation the next morning and be in a better state to decide what to do.

Food — what did we have? A fine large bag of oatmeal and a primus stove with paraffin, but no methylated spirits. Robin hadn't got a clue about primus stoves but fortunately I had. I seemed to remember that you surrounded the burner with methylated spirit, lit it, and when the burner was nice and hot you pumped up the pressure and hey presto! the paraffin vapour burst into a beautiful, clear, hot, sizzling flame. Using a little paraffin instead of methylated spirit I carried out this procedure several times until, wonder of wonders, the primus suddenly burst into life. No doubt experienced campers, boy scouts, girl guides, etc will laugh at this, but to me it was one of my greatest triumphs. Now for water: just cram one of the old saucepans full of snow and melt it; but what a lot of snow is required to produce a few inches of water (I believe that one inch of rain equals ten inches of snow). The water was heating up nicely, so now in with the oatmeal and, stirring vigorously, we ended up with a pot full of sticky, grey-looking porridge. We ate it really hot straight out of the pot, without sugar, salt or milk and it tasted marvellous. It was now getting on for 1830 and beginning to cool off a lot but, regretfully, we decided not to light the iron stove for fear of the wood smoke attracting unwelcome attention. The other huts we had seen were hidden from us by a small hill and one of these, we remembered, was quite large. They would obviously have to be investigated but we decided they could wait until tomorrow and that we should settle down where we were for the night. I took a final look out of the door — it was all so quiet, peaceful and lovely, but also desolate. There was still a slight haze of smoke drifting up from our poor old Skua, but apart from that nothing, just complete and utter silence. I shut the door and said to Robin, 'Let's get some sleep and tomorrow we'll get cracking'. Robin had been poring over his map again without success, and was ruefully folding it up when we heard a whistle blowing!

Encounter at Grotli

We had had a pretty busy day and I think our nerves were beginning to feel as though they couldn't take much more. To us a whistle close to 'our' hut could only mean one of two things — Germans or a Norwegian ski patrol. I said quickly to Robin, 'I'll slip out quietly and investigate and you stay here and keep quiet'. He nodded assent so I opened the door a little and squeezed silently out. There coming towards me up the slope leading to our hut was a tall, good-looking, youngish man in a smart grey uniform. He was on foot, not skis, and had a business-like small automatic pistol in a holster at his waist. Now at that time, silly though it sounds, I had never seen a Norwegian Air Force uniform or a German Luftwaffe one, and although I could see that he was wearing pilot's wings, I still didn't know whether he was friend or foe. Goodness knows what he was making of me, for I was in Royal Marine officer's blue uniform with thin red stripes down the trousers and also wearing wings, I'm sure he'd never seen the likes of me before, but no doubt would have recognized Robin as a naval officer as naval uniform is similar throughout the world.

There was no going back now and as we approached each other I heard more whistles blowing and in the distance saw two other figures in grey converging on us. The Partridge fatalistic calm was coming over me now and I knew that somehow I, and Robin, were going to have to bluff this out. We were only ten paces apart and what I feared was confirmed, as I could see German eagles on the lapels of his uniform. So we, unarmed, were out-numbered three to two by an armed enemy.

Then we were face to face. He smiled, and in the best continental fashion shook hands, turned and pointed to the other two approaching and now quite close, saying something in German. My German, save for yes and no, was absolutely nil and it was to transpire that none of them spoke a word of English. So there was very definitely a communications problem and looking back on it now I think that perhaps it was just as well. I don't know what Robin's thoughts were at this moment, for all that he could see from the hut was myself surrounded by three armed men in grey uniforms. I had to shake hands with the other two and I then beckoned them all towards our hut. We all entered, there was more hand-shaking with Robin, all very friendly, then we started to converse — in sign language! The first German I had met was a pilot and an officer and the other two were NCOs.

With signs the German pilot eventually got us to understand that they were three of a crew of four from a Heinkel that had been shot down by three Spitfires, that one of his crew, the rear gunner, was dead, and that one with him in the hut had a bullet through the elbow and was in great pain. Robin and I looked at each other significantly: we knew that the only single-engined monoplanes in the area were Skuas, and it was dawning on us that this was the surviving crew from the Heinkel we had shot down a few hours previously. I immediately went into a long pantomime of gestures indicating that we were the survivors of the crew of a 'Wellington bomber' that had crashed nearby with engine failure, and I tried to make it more convincing by drawing an aeroplane with two engines. My story sounded awfully lame to me but it appeared to be accepted, and all remained friendly.

I feel I must remark at this point on the efficiency and preparedness of the Germans. Here were Robin and I stranded in the wilds of Norway which was obviously something that might happen to any of our aircrews; and what did we have in the way of survival kit? — nothing. What did the Germans have? — emergency rations, first aid kit, automatic pistols, whistles and pocket compasses. If I had my time over again I would be carrying all that and a pair of snow-shoes as well!

Now, Robin and I alone in our little hut was one thing, but five of us, including three armed enemy, was quite another kettle of fish and I didn't like it at all. Something had to be done. I took Robin on one side, and laughing and joking from time to time in an attempt to make it appear as though our conversation was casual, told

The bullet-riddled tail section of the crashed Heinkel bomber.

him that I was going to try and get to the big hut and would he mind staying with the Germans. He said he thought it was a good idea and he didn't think the Germans would start anything because he was pretty certain they thought they were in Norwegian held territory. By sign language again I managed to get the German officer to understand that I was going to go to the other side of the hill and return shortly, and that Robin was going to stay with them. No objections were raised.

I set off towards the big hut and the going was relatively good. I walked round the small hill and there it was, not more than half a mile away and much bigger than we had thought. This was no hut, but quite a large building in the traditional Norwegian timber style. As I got near I saw telephone wires coming to the house and a huge great bomb crater 50 yards from it blackening the snow all around. It had obviously suffered a very near miss. A hundred yards further on and nearly there I came across a signpost which said GROTLI; now all we had to do was to find this on the map and we could pin-point our position. There was no sound coming from the building, no smoke and nothing to suggest it was inhabited. I couldn't hang around too long leaving Robin alone with his 'friends', so, summoning up courage, I walked up to the front door, pushed it open and entered.

I was in a small foyer with a desk counter on one side and a small display cabinet full of cigarettes on the other. I then guessed that this was a small hotel that had perhaps been quickly abandoned after the bombing. I let out a shout, in English of course, 'Anybody at home?' No reply, so I started to explore the ground floor a bit. I found the telephone and tried it; it was dead, and looking out of a nearby window I saw that the lines were down. That was a great disappointment but at least solved one of my problems — what to say if a Norwegian voice answered the 'phone and

The Grotli Hotel and the bomb crater.

couldn't speak or understand English. I had decided that all I could do was to use the international distress signal and repeat over and over again 'Mayday Grotli — Mayday Grotli'. I continued my exploration and found myself in the kitchen, which was stocked with food of all sorts: bacon, eggs, coffee, flour, biscuits and many other things. We were not going to starve in a hurry. I then had a quick look round the bedrooms upstairs: nobody there, the whole place deserted. I went back to the kitchen, selected one of those large square 4lb tins of mixed biscuits and on my way out pinched all the cigarettes from the display case. I had smoked the last of my own some time ago!

With my booty I now made my way back to poor Robin in the hut with the Heinkel crew, and was relieved to find that peace and amity still reigned. I told Robin about the hotel, made a present of the biscuits to the Germans and managed, I think, to make them understand that they were to stay in the hut and that Robin and I were going to go to the other side of the hill. Thank goodness there appeared to be no objections to this plan and maybe they were as glad to get rid of us as we were of them. As we left the German officer even made me a present of a packet of cigarettes from their emergency rations.

Robin and I chatted as we struggled towards the hotel and were both glad that it was not far to go. He told me that during my absence the Germans had been quite friendly and had talked a lot between themselves and that he had got the impression that they were beginning to doubt their own 'Spitfire' story. I then told him about the name Grotli and Robin said that it meant nothing to him and he only hoped such a small place would be marked on the map. I also said I hadn't mentioned it to the Germans lest it should have given them an indication as to whose territory we were in, German or Norwegian. As long as they thought we were in Norwegian territory I felt we were fairly safe and that there would be little likelihood of them making us prisoners, which of course they could quite easily do.

As soon as we arrived at the hotel we spread out the map and started anxiously searching for Grotli. Minutes ticked by and still no Grotli, until suddenly Robin put a finger on the map and said 'There'. Sure enough there was the name, and it was well outside Robin's previously estimated circle. Now at least we knew where we were but it didn't help all that much. We reckoned it was just still inside Norwegian-held territory but it looked terribly remote, 3000 feet up in the mountains and 20 miles or so from any proper town or village. We were no longer lost but we were still well and truly stranded.

Robin had a quick look round the hotel, upstairs and downstairs, and confirmed that it was empty. We then went down to the kitchen where to my joy I found that the large stove I had previously noticed was an oil-burner with wicks and that all I had to do to light a hotplate was to turn up the wick and apply a match. Robin made some excellent coffee and I found some biscuits, butter and cheese and we had a satisfying late evening snack. Well fed and warm now there was nothing more we could do, so, as nightfall was not far away and we didn't consider it safe to show any lights, the only thing to do was to go to bed. We went upstairs, chose the best double bedroom, took off our flying boots and jackets and, keeping the rest of our clothes on, lay down on the double bed under a beautifully down-filled continental quilt.

Looking back on the situation now I suppose we really ought to have arranged it so that one of us was on watch throughout the night whilst the other slept; not that we could have done much unarmed if we had heard somebody coming. We didn't think we would be able to sleep but at least we would get a good rest. As it was we both fell asleep almost instantly and I was the first to wake the following morning: it was daylight and looking at my watch I was astonished to see that it was 0800. I sprang out of bed, woke Robin, and said 'For goodness sake let's get some breakfast'. We looked out of the bedroom window to see once again the same beautiful and desolate scene: snow and mountains everywhere and not a sound or a movement. Down we went to the kitchen and I appointed myself cook (I was quite an adequate cook!) and asked Robin to make some more of his excellent coffee. We ended up with bacon and eggs (two each) followed by biscuits, butter and jam and lots of coffee. Having finished this glorious meal we pushed back our plates, looked at each other, and said — 'What the hell are we going to do?'

We couldn't stay where we were for ever, comfortable as it was, as we knew that fairly soon we would be overrun by the German advance. Our great problem was mobility, how to travel any distance across the snow without continually sinking. There were several outhouses around the hotel and I thought it possible that in one of them I might find some skis. Robin still had his naval binoculars with him and I asked him to go up to the highest point possible in the hotel and make a really good survey of the surrounding countryside in the hope of spotting something of use. While he was doing this I started to investigate the outhouses. The first one was firmly padlocked and I couldn't get in; the second was unlocked but the door opened outwards and I had a hell of a job clearing away the deep snow sufficiently to get it open, only to find it full of useless junk. With the third I had the same trouble with snow but inside I found a pair of skis. They were so old and frail, with no proper bindings, that I guessed they had been abandoned as useless: but beggars can't be choosers and I felt they would be better than nothing. They were all that I found, but on returning to the hotel with them I met an excited Robin who had also made a discovery. He had managed to get out onto the roof and with his glasses had spotted a snow-covered building about two miles away down the valley and he was pretty certain that there was a wisp of smoke rising from a chimney into the still sunlit air. He reckoned that it was a small farmhouse with a barn attached. This would obviously have to be investigated.

Robin had never been on skis in his life but I had had one fortnight of winter sports in Switzerland at the age of 16, so I was the obvious choice for the two mile trip down the valley and poor old Robin was going to be left behind again all on his own. I arranged with him that if I found everything all right at the supposed farm and there was help I would signal to him, probably by morse, heliograph fashion, if I could find a suitable mirror, or otherwise by semaphore, and that I would instruct him either to sit tight or to start trying to make his way to the farm. If I went into the farm and didn't re-appear within 15 minutes he was to assume the worst and act as he thought best.

I was outside the hotel trying a shuffle around on my ghastly skis with Robin watching me when to my dismay round the corner appeared the German Heinkel crew. When they joined us I explained to the pilot as best I could what I was going to do, pointing towards the distant farm. I was beginning to get the impression that they were not quite so friendly now, and his answer to my proposal was a 'No' with a shake of his head. He then pointed to the member of his crew who was not wounded, then to me, and then to the farm. After he had done this it suddenly dawned on me that he was saying that if I went to the farm one of his men was to go with me. This was indeed a complication we had never dreamed of; if I set off I had no means of stopping the German coming with me and God knows what problems that might cause at the farm. If I didn't go then there we would be, all five of us, cooped up again together but this time in the hotel. I looked at Robin and he solved the problem instantly by saying, 'Carry on to the farm, I'll be all right here with these two'. So I turned to the German pilot, pointed to his crewman, myself and the farm and gave him a thumbs up. He nodded agreement.

Off we set, an ill-assorted couple. I wasn't doing very well on my skis as I kept on losing one, but my German companion really was floundering and after I had gone some 200 yards or so I was beginning to outdistance him by 20 or 30 yards and thought that at this rate I was likely to arrive at the farmhouse well ahead of him. This comforting thought was rudely shattered by the vicious crack of two rifle shots, a cry from the German and a spurt of snow between my legs. I looked back to see the German collapsed motionless in the snow with an ominous spreading red stain, then looked up and around to see that we were surrounded by a ski patrol dressed all in white and that I was covered by five steadily-held rifles. There was another shot and the snow spurted up just alongside me. It must have been a warning because if they wanted to kill or hit me they could hardly miss at that range. I stood still with my hands up and as they approached me I heard Robin come storming out of the hotel having heard the shots. I let out a great shout to him to stand still and put his hands up, which thank God, he immediately did. You would have thought that my situation was just about as dire as it could get, but fate had even one more trick to play. There was suddenly the roar of an approaching aircraft and a Heinkel He 111 appeared fast at about 3000 feet and proceeded to machine-gun the lot of us. We all hit the snow regardless of nationality and remainded motionless until the sound of the aircraft faded into the far distance. Then we all got up except for the huddled grey figure in the snow with an ever-increasing crimson mark spreading around him. The fact that a German aircraft was attacking this area confirmed what I had thought, that we were in Norwegian-held territory, and that the ski patrol was Norwegian. I was obviously still an object of suspicion in my strange uniform and it was when I was searched and a two shilling piece was found on me that they began to think that I was English. Two of them apparently recognized the face of King George V on the coin. I was allowed to lower my hands and I think I managed to get them to understand that there were two more armed Germans at the hotel and that Robin was a friend.

We then returned to the hotel to find that other members of the patrol had captured the remaining two Germans who sensibly offered no resistance, and one of the Norwegians who spoke quite good English was chatting to Robin. I really felt sorry for the two Germans, their cup of woe was brimming over. There was the captain of the Heinkel crew with his aircraft lost, one crew member killed in the air and another shot dead almost in front of his eyes. He kept on asking me a question

The remains of the half burnt Heinkel, partly sunk through a melted snowdrift, being examined by the Norwegians.

A group of German soldiers at the grave of Heinkel crewman Hans Hauck near the Grotli Hotel.

over and over again and I think it must have been 'Why did they shoot him?' For some extraordinary reason I almost felt guilty and was sure he was blaming me. I, too, was appalled that he had been shot and when I got the chance I told the Norwegians in no uncertain terms that we did not shoot prospective prisoners of war. I was assured that he had drawn his automatic from its holster and appeared to be about to fire so that they had no choice but to shoot. Perhaps being unarmed was a blessing in disguise for me at that particular moment!

The last I saw of my two Germans was them being shepherded into one of the hotel rooms and an armed guard being placed outside the door. Robin and I were then taken to the farmhouse I had been trying to reach, riding on the back of the skis of two Norwegians. In this fashion we couldn't go very fast but at least we didn't sink. On arrival we found that it was indeed a farmhouse and barn and that it belonged to Mr Sevald Grotli, the owner of the Grotli Hotel, a noted and much respected man who had lived in the mountains all his life like his forebears before him. He was a fine, tough, rugged-looking man of about 40 and although he appeared to be a civilian he seemed to be firmly in command of everybody and everything. Apart from him there were many others, as this appeared to be one of the local mountain rendezvous of ski patrols and it was Mr Grotli who had seen the smoke from our burning Skua and reported it. Also there, to our astonishment, were three young Norwegian girls who turned out to be nurses and who had been retreating on skis across the mountains accompanied by two young doctors to escape the advancing Germans. One of these girls had a Norwegian father and a Scottish mother and had spent much of her life in Edinburgh; hence her English was perfect

The Norwegian ski patrol examine the wrecked Skua and its machine guns.

Outside Sevald Grotli's farmhouse the ski patrol and nurses, with Robin Bostock and author on the right, relax during lunch in the spring sunshine.

and our identities were now established without any doubt. We were eagerly questioned as to how far the Germans had got but couldn't help as most of our recent flying had been in the coastal areas. General opinion was that the Germans were getting very close and there was much discussion of what to do with us, the doctors and the nurses. It was finally decided that an armed patrol should be summoned to escort us to Stryn that night as no movement was possible by day. We were told that this patrol would bring spare skis for Robin and myself and we were asked if we could manage three miles over the mountains on skis that night. With the Germans close at hand we replied with a very confident yes!

We were looked after very well that day and I have an excellent photo of several of us, including the girls, having a midday meal at a table outside the farmhouse in lovely spring sunshine. Several of the patrol who had surrounded us had had a look at our Skua and were very interested in the four Browning machine guns in the wings which had not been touched by the fire. They wanted to know if they took them out whether they could be used on the ground. I had to say that I thought it unlikely because when used in the air they were cooled by the airflow rushing past them and if used on the ground I thought they might very quickly overheat, but that it was worth a chance.

The youngest looking of the girls came up to me and told me, in quite adequate

English, that her parents lived in Molde and asked whether I had flown over it recently and was it all right. As I have already related I had flown over it the day before and it was in flames from end to end. I couldn't bring myself to tell her this and said that when I had flown over it three days ago it was perfectly unharmed, which of course was true, I was just concealing the truth of my last flight.

There were many comings and goings from the farmhouse that day with Sevald Grotli apparently well in command. The telephone was still working and it was by phone that arrangements had been made for our escort that night. We were told that our departure was planned for 0100 and advised to get some rest during the evening. I was fast asleep at 0130 when I was woken up and told that there had been a change of plans. The escort had not turned up and it was considered unlikely that it would now do so. The latest news of the German advance was ominous and if we were going to complete our journey by night we would have to leave by 0200. This puzzled me because three miles even in bad conditions could hardly take most of the night. I raised this point with Sevald Grotli through the 'Edinburgh' nurse and got the shock of my life. I learned that one Norwegian mile equalled seven English miles so Robin and I were going to have walk 21 miles over the mountains in flying boots as there were no spare skis!

The party was to consist of the three girls, the two doctors, Robin and myself, and two young local Norwegians armed with rifles. As we had no skis the plan was that those on skis should proceed in single file thereby beating down a reasonably hard track and that this, combined with the night frost, should enable Robin and me to walk without sinking into the deep snow. It was a clever idea and, except very occasionally, it worked. I had gathered that the farmhouse was going to be abandoned as a ski patrol rendezvous or headquarters, but that Sevald Grotli was determined to remain on his farm, Germans or no Germans, and I believe he did so for the duration of the war.

10

The long way home

We set off at 0200 hours in single file with Robin and me bringing up the rear. Apart from a brief stop for a sandwich and a drink at a hut about halfway we kept going fast and steadily. Robin and I found it hard and exhausting work but were quite determined not to hold the party up or be left behind. I really did admire the three girls because it was a mighty long slog, uphill and downhill, and they never faltered, never slowed and always had a smile and a word of encouragement for us. As it turned out the journey was exhausting but uneventful and at 0730 we arrived at Stryn.

We were led in to a huge barn-like building which was crammed with men of all sorts, some in uniform and some in plain clothes. Many of those in uniform appeared young and untrained, and by no means at home with their rifles. This was not really surprising since I think I am right in saying that it was over 120 years since Norway had experienced a war of any sort, and its people would be the last to claim that theirs was a militaristic country and society. But when driven to it they could fight for their country and freedom, and the courage and determination of the Free Norwegians, who managed to escape the occupation, and of the underground movement were unequalled.

In one corner of this great barn was a large iron stove with a huge pot of coffee brewing on top of it. Following a most welcome warming cup the nurses, doctors, Robin and I were taken to a nearby farmhouse and given a typical great Norwegian breakfast. After this we were sent on by bus to Nordfjordeid, a distance of about 25 miles, where the local Norwegian military headquarters was situated. On arrival Robin and I were conducted to the commanding officer, a general, who received us most pleasantly but was a little disappointed that we really couldn't give him any information about the German positions. He was a harassed, worried man but was kind enough to thank us and England for the help we were trying to give his country. He of course knew that we had been up all night slogging our way across the mountains, and, on his insistence, we were led away to a bedroom with two beds to have a good sleep. As we approached our bedroom I noticed a sentry standing outside the next room and asked what he was doing. The reply was that they had a spy in there and that they were going to take him out and shoot him at any moment!

Robin and I were of course physically very tired but mentally alert and on edge.

We lay down gratefully on our beds but sleep just would not come, and after an hour or two of restlessness we decided that we couldn't lie there any longer. I therefore asked to see the general again and explained to him that we felt quite useless until we could get an aeroplane once more and could he please help us to get to England. He was most sympathetic and agreed that for us to fight again we must fly. He looked at his maps and said that the nearest British forces were at Alesund and the best way for us to get there would be by motorboat under cover of darkness. Alesund we had flown over several times during the past few days and knew as quite a large town and port at the tip of a long narrow isthmus, probably about 40 miles away as the crow (or Skua!) flies.

Towards evening we were driven by car to the little village of Folkestad that lay on a fjord and as darkness fell we embarked on a reasonably large motorboat with a small cabin. I guess our maximum speed was around 10 knots and estimated that our voyage was going to take several hours. The crew consisted of the skipper and two other fine Norwegian fishermen with unfortunately not many words of English between them. We had been chugging along for about 30 minutes and Robin and I were down in the cabin chatting and smoking when a shout from the skipper brought us up on deck at the double. Somebody had fired a Very light at us from the nearest shore about half a mile away and sure enough as we watched there came another, a two-star white light. The skipper wanted to know whether it was friend or foe and how he should answer. He appeared quite confident that we would know, whereas of course we hadn't a clue, and thought it quite likely that if we couldn't give the correct response a machine gun might open up on us, and it could be Norwegian, British or German!

I guessed the fjord was about two miles wide so I told the skipper to take a course down the middle and on no account were any lights to be shown, navigation or otherwise. Half an hour later, while proceeding about a mile from either shore, more Very lights appeared, but this time double red instead of double white! The skipper didn't like it at all, and neither did I, but I was determined to appear casual and asked him just to maintain course and speed. It was very nerve-racking waiting in this flimsy boat for guns to open up on us but happily that was our last scare and in the early hours of the morning we tied up at Alesund. We were taken to the Grand Hotel which lay quite close to the quay, shown to a very nice double room, and this time we really did sleep.

Noises in the hotel woke us about 0800 so we got up, washed and dressed, but couldn't shave or clean our teeth as we lacked razors and toothbrushes: we were beginning to feel and look pretty scruffy. We went down to the dining room and saw an extraordinary scene; the room was full of naval and marine officers and could well have been the wardroom of a shore establishment. We had a great breakfast with marvellous coffee that I simply could not stop drinking. After breakfast I sought out the senior British officer who turned out to be a major of Marines, and a very worried major he was too. I had met him before but didn't know him at all well. He explained that the situation was hopeless; the Germans were advancing rapidly in force, had complete mastery in the air and he had a mere two hundred marines with whom to defend Alesund. At the moment this force was inland at the neck of the isthmus and the best they could hope to do would be to fight a delaying action, but the major feared that if the delaying action was too successful then there was nothing to stop the German Air Force bombing Alesund into rubble with horrifying civilian casualties. He reckoned that the only hope for Alesund and its people was for the British forces to withdraw and to let the Germans advance unhindered; this he was unwilling to do if it meant his own forces surrendering without a fight, but because of Alesund's geographical position the only line of withdrawal was by sea. It was now that he dropped his real bombshell; he told me that he was not in contact with any British higher command because he had not got the correct code books or frequencies! So we were cut off and incommunicado, and that horrible hunted feeling began to creep over me once again.

During the morning Robin and I were shown round Alesund and its defences by the Norwegians. These defences were practically nil, and included a few anti-aircraft guns but no ammunition. We were proudly shown their anti-incendiary bomb precautions at the Post Office and communication HQ, a fine large modern building with a flat roof, on which had been spread about 12 inches of wet sand. This I thought was an excellent anti-fire device, but felt that the weight of it must have been colossal and prayed that the flat roof was really strong.

It was embarrassing to walk through the streets as girls and women would rush up to us and thank us for rescuing them from the Germans. They had yet to learn what I already knew — that as soon as we could find the means we were going to have to abandon them. The town was being bombed in a desultory fashion from time to time, and near the hotel I was shown a 1000 lb German bomb that had failed to go off; it was a menacing sight and not very encouraging. I comforted myself with the thought that Alesund was going to be a very useful port and town to the Germans and that they would probably try to capture it as undamaged as possible.

It was in a gloomy and unhappy frame of mind that I sat down to lunch with Robin and the major. During the meal we discussed with him how we could possibly establish communications, because once a message had got through explaining the hopelessness of his position the evacuation of his force could be carried out quickly and relatively safely at night by one destroyer. The major said that local Norwegian sources of information reported the assembly of a very large British force at Andalsnes but that he could not get in touch with them. Andalsnes lay some 60 to 70 miles east by north of Alesund at the head of the great Romsdalsfjord.

I had always been a great believer in the old service saying 'Never volunteer for anything, and never refuse to do anything', but I was now to break this very sound rule, and I told the major that if he could arrange a car and English-speaking driver, Robin and I would try to get through to Andalsnes and report that the evacuation of his force by sea must be carried out immediately if it was going to survive. He jumped at the idea! Within half an hour a car appeared outside the hotel and we were introduced to our chauffeur, a pleasant-looking young Norwegian in his early twenties who spoke good English, and who appeared willing and keen to undertake this journey. Robin and I were issued with a .45 service revolver each plus 20 rounds for each gun and I was given £20 in pound notes in case, for some reason or other, we needed money.

We set off quietly at about 1330 on a trip that I guessed was going to be no picnic,

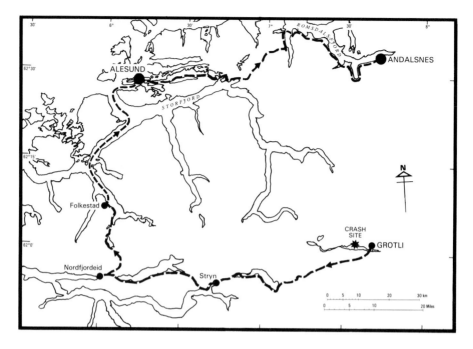

but anything was better than sitting in Alesund doing nothing, with the air raid sirens going frequently, and the odd bomb dropping with a nerve-shattering crash. Now we had a definite mission — to try and let the powers-that-be know that if they wanted their Alesund detachment back safely a sea evacuation must be arranged immediately.

The roads down at sea level were clear of snow but unfortunately were often unsurfaced. At times this could mean that if we went too fast a considerable cloud of dust was created which would be visible from the air. Fortunately most of the German bombers were flying quite high, seldom below 5000 feet, and as long as we could get reasonable warning of their approach we stood a good chance of being undetected. As flyers we knew only too well that it was the moving target which was so easily spotted and our plan was to stop at the first hint of danger, preferably in the shade if possible, as it was a bright, sunny day. We were in a saloon car and it is not easy to see up and around from that type of vehicle, but we did our best, Robin watching up and behind and myself up and in front. We didn't think the Germans would waste bombs on a small target like a single car but guessed that if we were spotted they would probably come down and machine gun us as they did up at Grotli.

It was a macabre game of hide-and-seek and we had to stop several times, twice under the cover of trees and twice in shadow; once a bomber appeared to spot us from about 6000 feet when we were on a very open stretch of road and there was no cover of any sort available. He passed over us, turned and started to head back towards us maintaining height. Robin exclaimed 'I think he's carrying out a bombing run'. We were out of that car like lightning and climbing frantically up a large hill to the left of the road to scatter into the cover of a wood. Robin was right, it was a bombing run! He dropped a stick of bombs which went off with deafening roars, but fortunately fell a hundred yards or so the other side of the road and clear of us. How I hate being bombed, and what a giant hammer to crack so small a nut. I guessed he was at the end of his mission, jettisoned his bombs on us and headed off to the south, probably back to northern Denmark, from where I believe their Heinkel He 111s were operating.

We returned to the car and went on with our journey; all went well until we came to an obstacle I was not expecting. If you look at a map of that part of Norway you will see that you cannot make many journeys by road without either making very long detours or crossing one, or sometimes more, fjords by car ferry, and that is what happened to us. We arrived at the Romsdalsfjord and according to our Norwegian driver we had to cross it to get to Andalsnes. We found the ferry but no sign of crew or any life at all. We could all drive a car and I could fly an aeroplane, but none of us could drive a car ferry.

There were some cottages not far from the quay and our Norwegian friend set off towards them to find out whatever was possible. He returned a few minutes later with the captain of the ferry. The captain was adamant; he was not going to take his ferry across the fjord; every time he tried he was shot up by German aircraft and he had had some very narrow escapes. This argument went on for some time and eventually I suppose you might say that we blackmailed him into agreeing, because we gave him to understand that the safety of Alesund and all its inhabitants depended on our getting to Andalsnes.

The fjord was fairly wide at this spot and the crossing would take the best part of 30 minutes during which there could be no hiding in shadows, but against this had to be balanced the fact that once over the other side we were very close to our objective.

The ferry started up and we drove on board. I think this was the worst part of the whole journey; I don't know how any of the others felt but I was just plain down-right scared. There was nothing to do except wait for an attack from which we would have no escape and no chance of surviving. We couldn't even try and fight back. Chug! Chug! Chug! Chug! The ferry went on steadily and slowly and we were just past the middle point (the point of no return) when from our starboard side we heard and saw four Heinkels at about 6000 feet surrounded by AA bursts and also the crackling sound of a very heavy AA barrage. To our astonishment around the headland about half a mile up the fjord from us came a large warship being bombed and fighting back with everything she had got. Robin immediately identified her as HMS *Coventry* which had been converted into an AA cruiser and was armed with 10 four-inch anti-aircraft guns. It was an awe-inspiring sight, this great ship at full speed crashing down the fjord with a huge bow wave and a foaming stormy wake. I was so enthralled by it that I believe I almost forgot to be scared for a moment or two. HMS *Coventry* passed 300 yards astern of our cockleshell and we rocked and tossed violently in her wake. She was still pursued by the Heinkels but they appeared very unwilling to press home a proper attack against the volume of fire directed at them. During this extraordinary incident we were still chugging doggedly towards the far shore and as *Coventry* disappeared down the fjord we safely reached the quay. The Heinkels didn't appear to be pressing their attack very vigorously and I got the impression that they were each waiting for one of the others to fly through the flak on a steady bombing run. Startling and frightening as this amazing incident was we probably owed our safe passage to it. Who was going to bother about our little vessel when there was such a prime alternative target?

The skipper of the ferry very wisely decided he was going to stay put until nightfall when he would try to return to the other side. We thanked him gratefully, bade good-bye and drove off the ferry to continue our journey. We were right about being quite close to Andalsnes as after 20 minutes driving we reached the outskirts of the town, and there we had to stop the car. The place had been heavily bombed and was a shambles, with great craters in the road and no chance of driving past them. What to do now? There was no sign of life, nobody from whom to ask directions and no indications of any military presence whatever. One thing we were not going to do, and that was return to Alesund, even if we could. We therefore decided to abandon the car and we tried to persuade our Norwegian driver to come along with us on foot. He however was completely and absolutely determined to return to Alesund and nothing we could say would persuade him otherwise. With many thanks we said good-bye and good luck and as he turned the car round Robin and I walked on down the ruined road.

We had been walking for about 20 minutes when two armed figures jumped out from behind a hedge and halted us. I wondered how much more of this sort of thing my poor old nerves could stand when, to my immense relief, I recognized them as a Lieutenant and Sergeant of my own corps, the Royal Marines. Fortunately they were not trigger-happy and instantly saw what we were, dishevelled naval and marine officers. The Lieutenant was a fine young chap, cheerful and competent, and seemed quite certain of what he was going to do and how he was going to accomplish it. He had been posted there with a platoon of marines as an outpost to watch for surprise attacks by German parachutists. He, of course, was able to direct us towards the headquarters of the main force which was waiting for evacuation by sea. His orders were to cover the evacuation in case of attack and not leave his position until everyone was embarked. But with a grin he told me he was going to make certain that neither he nor his men would be left behind.

We carried on down the road according to his directions and found an extraordinary sight. Among some scrubland near the edge of the fjord were hundreds, maybe a thousand or so, soldiers and officers sitting and lying under the bushes, and very good cover from the air they made. We were directed to headquarters where we found a general and his staff squatting under another clump of bushes. I reported to the general, explained what had happened to us and how we had got there, and also the problem of the detachment at Alesund. He wasn't too pleased and retorted that he had problems of his own, but he did agree to try and get a report through about Alesund. Robin and I then found a bush that wasn't too crowded and sat down, chatting to those around us. I learned that this force of ours had been ordered to retreat to the head of Romsdalsfjord at Andalsnes and await evacuation by sea. I also learned that a much superior German force had been following them up and was thought to be getting uncomfortably close.

The destruction of Andalsnes by German bombing during April 1940.

The general had covering forces a little further inland whose instructions were the same as those given to our lieutenant, to delay the enemy advance while the main evacuation took place and then, if possible, to fight a rearguard action back to the fjord and embark themselves. Whilst waiting, one of the great dangers was attack from the air, and a stick or two of bombs across this concentration of troops would have caused horrible casualties. The cover was good and unless there was any undue movement there was a fair chance that they would not be spotted by the odd Heinkel or two that appeared from time to time. One snag, however, worried me terribly; this force had one light Bofors anti-aircraft gun, obviously manned by a very keen and optimistic crew. Every time a Heinkel appeared even remotely in range they opened fire — with tracer ammunition! Now that could certainly attract an air attack and as the chance of this gun scoring a hit on high flying bombers was very remote it seemed madness to me that it should risk drawing attention to us. As a junior officer I hesitated to tell the general himself what I thought but managed to get hold of one of his staff officers and tell him that as a pilot I considered that this confounded gun should only open fire in the event of a definite attack. Thank goodness he agreed with me, told the general, and suitable orders were passed to the gun crew. It didn't open fire again.

Time was getting on, evening was not far away, and just as I was wondering whether we were going to have to spend the night under the bushes, I heard an excited exclamation and saw that those near me were pointing down the fjord. I looked up and saw the most magnificent and welcome sight I have ever seen. Two great City Class cruisers and five destroyers were coming up the fjord flat out. And how utterly efficient they were; I really felt proud to be connected with the Navy as a marine. As they got near and slowed two destroyers detached themselves,

HMS Manchester: 9400 tons, 700 crew, 32 knots, twelve 6 inch guns. This Southampton Class cruiser, seen here after the Norway campaign with its Walrus spotter plane forward of the second funnel, was eventually sunk while on Malta convoy in the Mediterranean on 13th August 1942.

continued towards us and adroitly came alongside the quay. The embarkation then started and had obviously been extremely well organized. Small parties of about platoon size would assemble and proceed towards the ships one after another. There was no panic, no rushing and no delay. Robin and I were detailed to join one of the first parties and when the destroyer had a full load it swung quickly away from the quay and headed for the nearest cruiser. When we were alongside we all swarmed aboard and I found that I was in HMS *Manchester*. The wardroom was a curious sight, full of army officers of all ages and ranks, most of them very tired and dirty. Food and drinks were available on a help-yourself basis, the Navy doing its bit really well even under these rather hazardous circumstances. The commander (Executive Officer) paid a brief visit to see that all was going well. He spotted me and very kindly put his cabin at my disposal as he knew that he was going to have to be up all night whatever happened.

The last of the main party had soon embarked and one of the destroyers was sent inshore again to bring off, and wait for if necessary, the rearguard parties. The whole force then swung down the fjord and headed for sea at full speed. Our main dangers now were air attack and submarines; speed was essential on both counts as a really fast-moving ship makes a difficult target for a submarine and the sooner we got close enough to the Scottish coast to be within range of our shore-based fighters the sooner the air threat would be cancelled out.

These Norwegian fjords are vast and I suppose the distance from Andalsnes to the open sea would have been about 50 miles. Halfway down the fjord a Heinkel appeared and every ship opened up with everything it had got and put up a terrific barrage. This Heinkel was not going to be denied and held a steady course towards us at about 10,000 feet. Soon he was hit and in flames and a great deep-throated roar of triumph went up from the ship's crew. As the stricken aircraft spiralled downwards a small figure detached itself and a parachute opened; the parachute itself was on fire and after a controlled descent of about 500 feet it suddenly collapsed and the figure hurtled downwards to be dashed to pieces on the shore of the fjord. This brought forth another great animal roar of triumph. Such is war.

Quelling nasty thoughts of the ships being chased by hordes of enemy aircraft far out into the North Sea, I retired to the bunk in the commander's cabin and didn't wake up until we were entering Scapa Flow next morning. We moored not far from my own ship, *Ark Royal*, which had returned to Scapa a day or two earlier, and after breakfast Robin and I were sent back to her by boat. Much rejoicing and congratulations ensued, many having given us up for lost or at best prisoners of war. After we had reported to the Commander (Flying) we were very generously given leave with instructions to pick up a new Skua at Donibristle on our way back. Donibristle was a naval air station in southern Scotland which specialized in maintenance and repair of aircraft.

Before we left *Ark Royal* for our leave I asked if it was known what had happened to the detachment at Alesund and was relieved to be told that a destroyer had been sent in at night and they had all been successfully evacuated. It would be nice to be able to claim that this was a direct result of our trip from Alesund to Andalsnes. It could have been, and it could also have been an evacuation planned and carried out quite independently. I never did find out.

11

Return to HMS Ark Royal

My log book records that on 23rd May 1940 Robin and I rendezvoused at RNAS Donibristle to collect a new Skua. This we did but only after some trouble with various senior and junior officers at the station over the machine allocated. The first Skuas had had recurring engine failures, resulting in some horrible crashes causing injuries or deaths. In fact at that moment one of my midshipman pilots was in hospital with a broken back as a result of one such crash. The trouble was soon diagnosed and quickly cured by a not too complicated engine modification. But when I was checking over the new Skua at Donibristle I spotted that this particular modification had not been carried out and I refused to accept it as servicable for operational use. There was a hell of a row in which I pointed out that the type of flying we were doing was dangerous enough without the added risk of engine failure. They retorted that there was a war on (as if I didn't know), that aircraft were scarce and etc. As you can imagine Robin was more than one hundred per cent with me for he too would have to fly in it, and eventually, after an acrimonious fore-noon's delay, a modified Skua was produced and at 1405 Robin and I took off for Hatston, arriving there safely after an uneventful flight of 1 hr 45 mins.

Our stay at Hatston was pleasant but remarkably brief, one day in fact. *Ark Royal* and a strong force including the carrier *Glorious* had been ordered to proceed to the Narvik area in north Norway, well inside the Arctic Circle, to cover the withdrawal of British forces and shipping. So you see I was now about to head even further north. During the voyage there were sporadic attacks by odd Heinkels and once four appeared to be headed directly for *Ark Royal*. The ship opened fire with its 4.5 inch heavy artillery guns at what I thought was a vast range and the resulting shell bursts were not really very close to the aircraft, but were apparently sufficient to deter them from pressing home an attack and they veered off and disappeared. Apart from the occasional incident like this our passage was uneventful and we arrived off the island of Hinnöy on the morning of 4th June.

Then started four days of fighter patrols over Narvik, usually flying in flights of three aircraft. At this time of the year well up in the Arctic Circle there was no darkness at all and it was quite common to do a four hour flight starting at midnight followed by another one starting at midday. It was hard work for everybody, aircrew and ground crews, and also for the ship continually going to flying stations in order to fly aircraft on or off.

I have a vivid and unforgettable memory of Narvik, one of bleak forbidding splendour. The Ofotfjord leading up to the town was between forty and fifty miles long, the first half being relatively narrow, about two miles wide, then opening out to as much as ten or twelve miles in places. There was a narrow strip of low ground round most of the fjord, then the rock rose quite steeply to about 1500 feet or more. The town of Narvik itself lay almost at the head of the fjord and here the scenery was even more spectacular, the high ground coming down to the town and rising up behind it to well over 3000 feet. The sun didn't shine much whilst I was there and everything looked dark, black and menacing save where the snow still lay. To start with, as I flew up the fjord on patrol, I could see nothing; no movement, no sign of life, just utter desolation. However, as I neared Narvik I saw ships, or parts of ships, because the shores of the fjord were littered with the masts, superstructure, and funnels of sunken shipping. This to me was more depressing than simple desolation. There is something infinitely sad about a 'wounded' or 'dead' ship.

My four days of patrolling in the Narvik area were completed without incident and on the fifth day the large convoy of ships had loaded stores and men and the evacuation was complete. We all headed south, and my next three days flying consisted of protective fighter patrols over the convoy. We usually kept two sub-sections of three always in the air and I was averaging eight hours flying in every 24, in two trips of roughly four hours. On the second day a shadowing Heinkel recklessly got a little too close and was caught by the patrolling Skuas and shot down.

When these aircraft landed-on they reported that the Heinkel had crash-landed in the sea and that its crew was alive and afloat in a rubber dinghy. They also reported the position of the dinghy which was some distance from the convoy and made it quite clear to the Commander (Flying) that they, and all other aircrews, expected them to be picked up and not abandoned in the North Sea. The Commander went to the Captain and the Captain went to the Admiral. The Admiral apparently was not unsympathetic but said that submarines had been reported in this area and he was not going to risk a ship and its whole crew to rescue four Germans. He did add, however, that if and when the situation allowed he would detach a destroyer to pick them up. I never did find out whether or not they were saved.

I must mention here the Hurricane squadron which had been operating under appalling conditions from a frozen lake in Norway. With the impending evacuation of all British forces they were faced with abandoning their aircraft or flying them out and landing on *Ark Royal* or *Glorious*. Landing on either carrier presented problems that many thought were insurmountable. It was not a Fleet Air Arm squadron but a Royal Air Force one; the pilots had never deck landed or had any deck landing training; added to which the Hurricane was not equipped for deck landing, having no hook to catch the arrestor wires and so bring the aircraft to a rapid stop. They would have to rely on superb airmanship, judgment and brakes. To their everlasting credit they elected to have a go and all aircraft landed safely without even the slightest damage. Sadly it was to no avail.

On the following day *Glorious* began running short of fuel for its aircraft and was thus not in a position to carry out its main fighting role. It was therefore decided to detach the carrier and an escort of two destroyers with orders to proceed direct to Scapa Flow. The next heard from *Glorious* was a signal from her to Flag Officer

(*Ark Royal*) saying 'Two PB's ----', and ending abruptly. The story has been told elsewhere in detail of how they were intercepted by *Scharnhorst* and *Gneisenau* and how *Glorious* and her two escorts were sunk fighting to the last in the finest naval tradition. I haven't the knowledge to add anything to those excellent accounts already written but feel compelled to mention the irony of fate that allowed twelve RAF Hurricane pilots to land their aircraft safely and brilliantly on an aircraft carrier's deck only to die a seaman's death the following day. Indeed, someone, somewhere, works in mysterious ways.

12

Disaster at Trondheim

The sinking of *Glorious* and her escorting destroyers was a terrible blow to all of us. We were depressed by the dreadful loss of life and many of us lost numerous personal friends. Back in the corridors of power an immediate decision must have been made that the loss of *Glorious* should be instantly avenged, and my guess is that somebody recalled the success of the Skua dive-bombing on the *Königsberg* in Bergen harbour.

The next thing that happened to me was that I was summoned by Commander (Flying) and taken to see the Admiral. The Admiral told me briefly and succinctly that he intended to send both Skua squadrons into Trondheim harbour to attack the German Fleet and asked for my comments. Now had I been able to say truly what my immediate reaction was I might have said something like: 'Whoever thought this one up must be absolutely bonkers, I'm not going and neither are any of my squadron!' But of course one doesn't and can't say that sort of thing, although with hindsight perhaps one should have. But I did say that I hoped nobody was comparing this with the *Königsberg* raid for the following reasons: there were now 24 hours of daylight and thus no night cover, clear skies and no cloud cover; and furthermore Trondheim lay 45 miles up-fjord or, if the islands Fröya and Hitra were counted as mainland (from which we might be observed) then it was 80 miles inland, and there was no chance of getting there undetected, intelligence reports having made it absolutely clear that the target was well protected by German Messerschmitt Me 109s and 110s.

I paused in my appreciation of this proposed operation as I observed that the Admiral was looking pretty grim, and wondered if at any moment he would charge me with 'lack of moral fibre', the Services' wonderful euphemism for cowardice: but he said nothing and I finished up by adding that unless we could have fighter cover or diversionary air action of some sort the operation could not succeed and he would have unacceptable losses. He smiled and said he agreed with me, then revealed that a diversionary attack on Vaernes airfield by Bristol Beauforts had been arranged, and that he had decided both Skua squadrons should take off at midnight, with a view to attacking at 0200 hours. I felt I could say no more.

Commander (F) told me to work out plans for the attack with Lieutenant Commander John Casson, the commanding officer of 803 Squadron, who as the senior squadron commander would be leading the attack, and for us both to arrange for the briefing of air and ground crews. I found a grim-looking John in the wardroom and apparently the Admiral had seen him before me. We compared notes and found that we had each told the Admiral roughly the same, except that John had said losses of at least 50 per cent should be expected, to which the Admiral replied that he thought this was being a little pessimistic.

It was approaching midday when John and I went in to lunch and had rather a subdued meal. Afterwards we set about planning, being joined by my observer, Robin Bostock, and John's observer. As soon as we got our heads together and considered the problem it became clear that there was not really much planning that could be done. We would have liked to approach the target unseen, but with no cloud or darkness the only way this was possible was at ground level. Such an approach would then require a slow climb to dive-bombing height near the target, for the Skua's rate of climb with a full load was indeed slow and we would be easy meat for marauding enemy fighters. No, the only chance was to go in high, hope the Beauforts would be there, and in the confusion slip through and carry out our attack. We also decided that if there was no diversion and we were being attacked we would break formation and all aircraft would act individually, selecting the best and biggest targets available. There was to be no rendezvous point, all aircraft would be given a course back to the ship from Trondheim and if necessary would have to find their own way. We decided to cross the coast at 12,000 feet, losing height from there on to arrive at Trondheim at about 8000 feet. Not a very brilliant plan but there seemed to be no alternative. We had a preliminary briefing of aircrews at 1630 that afternoon, with final briefing to be at 2300 hours. Checking aircraft and aircrew availability John and I decided to take nine aircraft from his squadron and eight from mine, making a total of 17.

Now began a very long and very demoralizing wait. Commander (F) had told me that if for any reason the Beauforts were unavailable the Admiral had given orders that our operation was to be cancelled. So there was still hope! I went round the hangars and chatted to the ground crews preparing our machines, trying to appear nonchalant and unperturbed. They were obviously doing their usual excellent job and I returned to the wardroom for a cup of tea, and had only that, having little appetite. Common sense told me that I ought to get some sleep, or at least a rest, so I went down to my cabin only to find that sleep was out of the question and that lying on my bunk just 'resting' wasn't exactly a soothing occupation either. I then thought of writing a sort of last letter to home and girl-friend but decided that his was a bit melodramatic and perhaps even courting disaster by anticipation. I ended up by returning to the wardroom and chatting to others who I assume were as apprehensive as myself but concealing it remarkably well; there were even a few who appeared genuinely belligerent and raring to go. When the bar opened I must admit that there was a temptation to have a few quick strong ones, but I was determined to resist for three very good reasons: drink and flying don't mix; as squadron commander I obviously had an example to set; and lastly I reckoned that any 'Dutch courage' taken on board would more than have evaporated after a two hour flight to Trondheim. So I went to the bar and ostentatiously ordered a large lemon squash.

Time, however, was passing painfully slowly. It was now 2000 hours, and I insisted that all my aircrew, including myself, had a light meal whether they felt like it or not. The time gap between lunch and our return to the ship at about 0415 was a long one and it would have been absurd to try to do an arduous and testing job on an empty tum. Actually I ate more than I expected and quite enjoyed it. Some good strong coffee followed and I think we all felt much better and were getting in the right sort of mood to do our very best.

At 2300 hours all aircrews were assembled for final briefing. The operations room informed us that the diversionary bombing raid had been arranged and confirmed, so we would just have to do the best we could and get on with it. Everybody was very calm and efficient and I don't think any casual observer could have detected the slightest sign of apprehension or doubt. After briefing John and I sent the aircrews down to the hangar to supervise final preparations on their own aircraft and to accompany them to the flight deck when they were ranged up.

It was at 2350 that the first of my aircraft sprang into life with a roar, quickly followed by the others. I was airborne at 0001 hours on the 13th June 1940 (rather an ominous date), the last of my squadron to take off, so that those already in the air

Range of Skuas of 800 and 803 Squadrons aboard HMS *Ark Royal* immediately before the Trondheim raid.

could form up on me as I climbed away from the carrier. We circled in formation waiting for John Casson, the last off, to be joined by his squadron, then both squadrons swung round on a course for the Norwegian coast and Trondheim. We climbed steadily in open formation until we reached a height of 12,000 feet. The weather was good, too good, with a completely clear sky, and maximum visibliity. We now settled down to our most economic cruising speed of 140/150 knots which would only be varied later by John Casson's observer's navigation requiring a higher or lower speed to arrive over the target at exactly 0200. At that moment I liked to think that there were also a dozen or so Beauforts well on their way from Scotland and also navigating to arrive precisely at that time.

We had been airborne now for well over an hour and ahead of us I could see the first land which Robin told me was the northern end of the island of Fröya. All aircraft were nicely in position and so far we had seen nothing, neither ship nor plane. As we passed over the island, in this very clear visibility, I could see a light-house and thought it highly probable that the Germans would have an observation post there to give good warning of any attack by sea or air. Now we were crossing over the mainland coast proper and there, confound it, was another lighthouse or coastguard station. I couldn't help but believe that the wires back to Trondheim were humming with the news that an enemy bombing force was approaching, and I could imagine the alarm being sounded at the aerodrome with Me 109s and 110s being scrambled one after another.

John Casson now started to go into a shallow dive, our speed building up to about 200 knots, and I asked Robin how far there was to go. He said he reckoned we were about 25 miles from Trondheim and that we should arrive there in about 10 minutes almost exactly at 0200. So far, so good. I was looking anxiously ahead for AA bursts in the air which would mean that the Beauforts were there and I hoped creating havoc with the Messerschmitts at Vaernes airfield. But as yet the air was as clear and still as ever. Speed was now building up to 240 knots, height 9000 feet, as John Casson manoeuvred to arrive over target on time and at the pre-arranged height.

I looked at my watch — it was three minutes to our deadline. There ahead of us I could see quite clearly the town of Trondheim and lying in the fjord the German fleet. I call it a fleet because it appeared to me that there were dozens of ships, including two larger ones that I assumed to be *Scharnhorst* and *Gneisenau,* which were obviously to be our targets if we could reach them. There was still no sign of the Beauforts and I think it was at that moment that John Casson and I knew we would have to go it alone, as we had always suspected.

Then the German AA fire opened up. I think only those who have experienced it can appreciate the volume of fire that a concentration of warships, supported by a considerable number of shore batteries, can put up, and can understand when I describe this barrage as intense with tracer bullets floating upwards and past us in thick showers. John Casson swung away to port putting his aircraft in open line astern and I did the same to starboard. As I did so I saw a twin-engined Me 110 flash past us heading for the other squadron and shortly afterwards a Skua spiralling downwards in flames. We were going to be sitting ducks for these Messerschmitts and I wondered how many of us were ever going to be able to get into a proper dive-

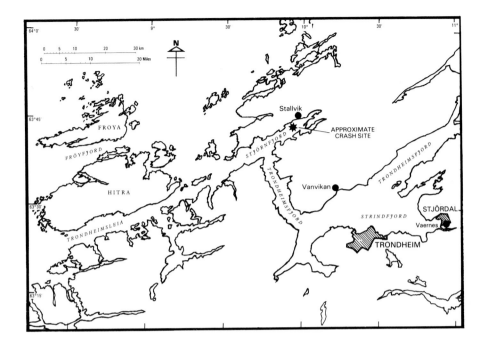

bombing position to drop an accurate bomb. Robin suddenly said 'Me 109 port quarter', and I took violent evasive action so that he shot past and under us. As I pulled round in a very tight turn I could see that all the Skuas of both squadrons were scattered and acting independently and that there were 109s and 110s all over the place. I saw one Skua carrying out what appeared to be a beautifully controlled dive-bombing attack on the further large ship but also had a fleeting glance of his dive getting lower and lower until he hit the water at full power with a horrible crash.

I asked Robin if there was anything on our tail and he replied 'No'. I decided that it was now or never and that if I was going to get into position to attack I must sacrifice some height in order to build up my speed on the run in. I put the nose down into a medium dive and headed at 260 knots towards the nearest pocket battleship. At just under 6000 feet I was in a position to attack, pulled up to lose speed and came off a stall turn with flaps down into a dive. This dive was started lower than I would have liked and the AA fire coming from the ship was indescribable. At 1700 feet I released my bomb and, veering violently to port, flaps now raised, continued on down to sea level and headed away across the fjord. Poor old Robin, who must have been having kittens in the rear cockpit whilst all this was going on, now reported that we had had a near miss ahead of the enemy ship and also that at the moment there was nobody on our tail though he had seen two more Skuas crash into the water. After five minutes of flying at zero feet we were well clear of the target area but by no means out of danger. Robin and I had often discussed what to do in this sort of situation. Flying at water or ground level offered the best chance of concealment but little chance of survival if we were attacked by superior forces and the aircraft was hit. Flying at any height from 1000 feet upwards offered less chance of concealment but an obvious chance of baling out. We had both agreed to opt for the chance of baling out and so I was now beginning to climb to gain height. We had reached 3000 feet when Robin said, 'Aircraft slightly above — port bow', and a quick glance showed a single engined seaplane of all things about to cross in front of and slightly above us. I eased back gently on the stick to raise my nose and as he passed in front of me and slightly above I got in a quick burst with my front guns. This may have been a big mistake on my part; either he hadn't seen me or he had mistaken me for an Me 109. At any rate his reaction to my burst of fire was a violent diving turn back towards Trondheim and that was a direction in which I was not going to chase him although even a Skua could have overtaken such an aircraft without too much trouble. But not only did he turn towards Trondheim, he also fired a four-star white Very light similar to the one fired by the submarine we had caught on the surface at Larvik. This could either have been the German recognition signal of the day or it could equally well have been a signal indicating the presence of hostile aircraft.

After this little incident we were at 4000 feet, about 20 minutes flying away from Trondheim and not all that far from the coast. I was just beginning to think that we had got away with it when over the intercom Robin said quietly, 'Two 109s coming up fast astern.' This was the dreaded situation we had often anticipated and had been frightened even to imagine, it scared us so much. We both knew that, barring some sort of miracle, we had really had it this time. Inexplicably, as far as I was concerned, I felt no fear or panic, merely my usual fatalistic calm and a determination to give them a run for their money. Had it been only one Messerschmitt we were dealing with it is just possible we might have got away with it, but two gave us no chance at all. The Me 109 was at least 80 mph faster than we were, was more manoeuvrable and was armed with cannon. In spite of this I had a trick or two up my sleeve and felt that if we could survive long enough and at the same time work our way out to sea we could possibly get rid of them; for I knew that shore-based fighter pilots never relished too much flying over water out of sight of land. If we could somehow remain in one piece till we were 50 miles off shore I felt there was a chance that they might give up the chase.

I felt terribly exposed sitting high up in the Skua's cockpit, with large expanse of windscreen in front of me which was not bullet-proof. Neither was there any armour under my seat or at my back and the large petrol tanks were not even self-sealing if hit. Robin of course was equally unprotected and had the unnerving view of every attack as it came with only a single Vickers K machine gun to defend us from stern attacks. The odds surely were stacked against us!

I have spoken before of the Skua's great, big, strong flaps that helped to make it such a good dive-bomber. I now planned to use these flaps to help avoid the approaching attacks at the same time working my way towards the sea. As soon as Robin shouted they were about to attack in line astern 'Now!' I went into a 45 degree dive and when they opened fire as my speed built up to 250 knots I suddenly put my flaps down. The result was instant, dramatic and very uncomfortable! We decelerated violently and at the same time shot straight up 500 feet or so and the attacking 109s passed underneath us. It speaks a lot for the ruggedness and strength of the Skua that it could stand this sort of treatment, while I continued to work my way towards the coast. Three times the 109s repeated this type of attack unsuccessfully and I was wondering how long it was going to be before they realized they would have to change their tactics. Unfortunately not very long....

Robin suddenly said 'One attacking from astern and one on starboard beam'. This was decidedly awkward and meant that my 'flap' tactic could make me an easy target if the aircraft on the beam waited until I had avoided the stern attack. So this time I did a really tight turn to starboard and managed to get a quick head-on burst at my beam attacker. Of course this left me more vulnerable to the stern attack and I could see his tracers going past me. I was still working my way towards the coast but our enemies' performance was so superior that they could attack, climb away, circle round and attack again. It couldn't last.

Robin had just said again, 'Attack astern and abeam' when I felt a thud that shook the aircraft and a large piece about the size of a soup plate came away from my starboard wing. It was probably a cannon shell but as it was outboard of the ailerons I still had control of my aircraft. They were circling and climbing ready for another attack — but this time there was no warning of firing from Robin. Suddenly the petrol tank behind my instrument panel, only a foot or two from my lap, went up in a roar of flames. From then on my actions were essentially reflex and must have been carried out at lightning speed.

I can remember slamming back my cockpit hood and the resulting slipstream drawing a great sheet of flame up between my legs, across my face and out of the cockpit; I can remember hitting the quick-release of my fighting harness, and then the next thing I was aware of was a violent and painful yank at my crotch. Inconsequentially I thought: 'That will teach you not to have your parachute harness properly and tightly adjusted!' and there I was at 3500 feet floating down with an Me 109 heading straight for me. As I was bracing myself for him to open fire he swerved to one side and was away. I looked around for another parachute — there was none. What had happened to Robin? Had he been killed in that last attack on us? Had he been unable to get out? Or was he still in the Skua now spiralling downwards and thinking it was brilliant evasive action I was taking? The Skua hit the fjord below and disappeared in a cloud of spray and wreckage. Robin, my observer, friend and good companion in many good and bad times was dead, but exactly how and when he died we shall never know.

I was now at 2000 feet and floating down gently in complete silence. I looked down and saw that I was heading for the centre of a fjord. It wasn't the main Trondheim fjord but an offshoot: even so it appeared to be a mile or two wide. I know the theory of being able to guide a parachute by pulling on the shroud lines, but I tried this with no effect at all other than nearly to collapse the canopy. Gently I drifted down: at 500 feet I was still heading slap for the middle of the fjord. I removed my flying boots and let them drop into the water then, in order to avoid getting tangled up in the parachute, at about 15-20 feet I turned and hit the quick-release buckle and dropped into the water. As I went under I felt a great searing pain as the salt water came into contact with my burnt face. With my Mae West flotation waistcoat on I soon popped spluttering to the surface and surveyed my situation. From eye level a few inches above the water's surface either shore of the fjord appeared to be miles away and I knew I'd never make it swimming. I also knew that with my flotation waistcoat on I wasn't going to drown. God knows why or how, I was still alive but apparently destined to die of exposure in the icy waters of this remote and isolated Norwegian fjord.

I had been swimming for about 20 minutes, getting very weak and the shore I was aiming for appeared as far away as ever. Self-preservation is a great spur and I guess I was going to go on swimming until I could swim no more. Suddenly I heard noises that sounded very like those made by oars in rowlocks and looking over my shoulder saw the bows of a small rowing boat bearing down on me. I was too far gone to feel any of the things I ought to have felt, like joy and relief at being rescued at last. I was mentally and physically drained and exhausted and I suspect in a state of deep shock as well. The boat was quickly alongside me and I was seized by the arms and seat of my trousers by two men, hauled on board, thrust into the bottom of the boat and covered quickly and completely with a tarpaulin. As I lay there, gasping and shivering in the dark, I was conscious of the boat being rowed rapidly back to the shore. The boat grounded, I was uncovered, helped out and half carried, half dragged to a farmhouse nestling close to the fjord shore. I had been rescued by two Norwegian fishermen from the farm who had rowed out to me, well knowing that anything moving on land or water was inviting machine gun attack from the air. To these two gallant men I undoubtedly owe my life.

My memories of the next forty-eight hours are vague and hazy. I can remember being stripped and rubbed down in the farm kitchen and being dressed in borrowed clothing which included a fine knitted traditional Norwegian cardigan. I can remember being examined in a Norwegian doctor's surgery for broken bones or other injuries but can't remember how I got there. It was he who dressed and bandaged my burnt face and gave me a warm drink from a cup with a spout as my lips were too painful for normal drinking, and I think it must have been this doctor who decided that my presence must be reported to the Germans so that I could get proper medical treatment. Fortunately, when my cockpit went up in flames I had had my goggles down and this protected my eyes and saved me from certain blinding. So, save for a burnt face I was still in remarkably good physical condition and had a long and restful night in the farmhouse.

The next day a car pulled up at the farm with three German NCOs and I was handed over to them and driven away. This was the start of five years, all but one month, as a prisoner of war.

13

Prisoner of War

It is not my intention to dwell long on my time as a PoW. Compared with some it was comparatively uneventful and I certainly could never compete with such spendid books as *The Colditz Story, The Great Escape, The Wooden Horse,* etc. There are certain moments and incidents, however, which are memorable to me and I think worth describing.

I feel I should start with the drive away from my good friends at the farmhouse. My escort were young, pleasant looking, efficient German NCOs but irritatingly confident and cocky. We drove for some time and came to Trondheimfjord at Vanvikan, I think. Here we had a long trip across the water by ferry to Trondheim which took us right through the German fleet. As far as I could see not a single ship had been damaged in any way whatsoever. This was a bitter blow to me, especially as I was later to learn that of the seventeen Skuas which had set out from *Ark Royal* only five had returned. This meant that this ill-conceived operation had cost twelve aircraft with their experienced aircrew for no result at all. No wonder my captors were cocky.

In Trondheim I was interrogated; but please do not put a modern interpretation on the word 'interrogated'. There was no intimidation, torture, electric shocks or even threats and shouting, and my insistence on giving only my name and rank was respected. After interrogation I was taken to a PoW cage set up on a hill just outside town. This was full of men of all the nationalities you could think of, for most of the inmates were from crews of British and allied merchant ships captured by the Germans. I can well remember having my face dressed and treated by a rather clumsy German medical orderly and being watched closely by a huge great negro. I thought he was just taking a gruesome interest until he saw me wince, then he came and held my hand and made comforting noises. I was very touched.

Next day found me under escort at Trondheim railway station where I was joined by two RAF officers and a pilot from John Casson's squadron. We were kept apart from the rest of the crowd while waiting for the train to Oslo and I suspect I was a pretty sorry sight with my face swathed in bandages, though I was now back in my uniform which had been dried, but hardly looked smart after its soaking in the sea. Suddenly there was a slight commotion among a crowd of nearby Norwegians and a middle-aged woman thrust herself through our escort, seized my hand, kissed it,

**Focke-Wulf Fw200B Condor transport of KGrzbV 105 during the Norwegian campaign.
The Condor was used to fly troops and supplies to Norway and take PoWs to Germany.**

and managed to give me a packet of cigarettes before being beaten off by the guards.

The journey to Oslo was long and uneventful and in happier circumstances I could have enjoyed the magnificent scenery we passed through. Although the train was crowded we had a compartment to ourselves simply because our escort had walked into an already crowded compartment and peremptorily ordered everybody out. On arrival at Oslo station we were driven by lorry to what I think was the Norwegian Police headquarters but which had been taken over and occupied by the German military. Here we were taken in front of a high-ranking German officer commanding the Oslo area. He was a stern forbidding-looking man and everybody (including me) appeared to be terrified of him. Through an interpreter he asked me as senior officer if we had any complaints as to our treatment. I replied that we were all commissioned regular officers and had the right to be treated as such under the Geneva Convention and not to be confined with other ranks of all sorts as had happened in the PoW cage at Trondheim. That really made him blow his top, but I think the full force of his reply was rather spoilt by having to be translated into English by his terrified little interpreter. This reply was that we were being treated in the same way as our brave allies, the French, were treating German officers; he had recently heard a rumour that the French were now shackling German officers, and if this was confirmed then we would be shackled too!

We were then led away to a large cell-like room with a high, barred, unreachable window overlooking the road. I mention this window because each evening of the two days we were there we would hear a low whistle from the road and a packet of

Norwegian cigarettes came lobbing through. Some brave Norwegian sympathizer was risking a lot to bring us comfort and encouragement, but we never found out who it was. We spent two days in our cell during which I was taken to a hospital ship in the harbour where my burns were treated by a very pleasant German army doctor who spoke good English. He told me that I had extensive second degree burns but that they should heal in a month or two and he didn't think that there would be any permanent scarring. The doctor was very proud of his hospital ship which he explained to me had been converted from one of the *Kraft durch Freude* (Strength Through Joy) holiday ships.

Our next move was on the evening of the third day when we were taken to Oslo airport and put on board a Focke-Wulf Condor, a huge four-engined long range reconnaissance aircraft — most impressive! There was a crew of four or five and four armed guards to keep an eye on us, two sitting in front facing us and two behind. There was obviously going to be no chance of us hijacking the aircraft and if we had I doubt if any of us could have flown it; I certainly couldn't! That night we flew at a great and very cold height to Frankfurt-on-Main, landing in the small hours of the morning in the middle of an air raid! We were driven to the nearby PoW camp *Dulag Luft* (German abbreviation for Transit Camp Air), through which all flying PoWs were processed before being sent on the the *Stalag Luft* (Permanent Camps Air). Here we four were separated and placed in different rooms in the German administrative buildings outside the compound. My room had a bed, chair and table and a very securely barred window. I was allowed to sleep away what remained of the night and was interrogated again next morning. Once more

In the lower bunk at Dulag Luft; the lighting gives an unexpected fireside effect.

this was in the 'correct' manner and no pressure was put on me to reveal anything other than rank and name. In fact I will take this opportunity to state that in general my treatment as a prisoner of war during nearly five years was always correct, even if a little unsympathetic at times.

My next move after this questioning was to a nearby German military hospital; I think it was a kind of convalescent hospital for servicemen. Here one upper floor had been reserved for wounded prisoners and I was one of a dozen or so British flying crew who had been shot down and could be classed as 'walking wounded'. I had no complaints except that none of the doctors seemed to speak English and there was a dire lack of interpreters. The food was good and reasonably plentiful and we were allowed to exercise in the rather pleasant grounds surrounding the building, but under armed guard. I was to stay six weeks in this hospital and it was during this time that I managed through the Red Cross to get the news home that I was a PoW. After the Trondheim raid I had been posted officially as 'Missing' so it was six weeks later before my family and friends finally learned that I was alive but a prisoner. After this period I was passed fit and returned to *Dulag Luft,* where I stayed for the best part of a year, about the end of which time I made my one and only escape.

The population of the camp varied greatly, as prisoners arrived, were processed, and then passed on to the permanent camp in northern Germany near Lübeck. There were however about sixteen of us who had managed to make ourselves almost permanent there as administrative staff, I as sports officer organizing games and exercise. It was decided that this so-called permanent staff should dig a tunnel designed to surface well beyond the nearest guard tower, and after about nine months hard and dirty work this was completed. There were, I think, about seventeen of us to go but only one of this party could speak fluent German and obviously he had by far the best chance of reaching and crossing the Swiss border. It was therefore decided that he should escape one night earlier than the main party, thus giving him 24 hours before the general hue and cry was raised, and this is how it was done.

Adjoining our main compound was our exercise field surrounded only by a single barbed-wire fence. When we were allowed to use this its perimeter was patrolled by armed guards on foot and when it was not in use they were withdrawn. But inexplicably, at any rate to me, this field had a permanent resident in the form of a very fierce billy-goat who had a little shed in which to sleep and shelter. He was a mighty ferocious fellow and had caught many a new unsuspecting prisoner up the backside with one of his charges. Now in his shed had accumulated a very considerable heap of goat dung, and the plan was to bury our German-speaker under this heap so that when night fell he would be able to crawl out, cut his way easily through the single wire fence and be well on his way to Switzerland. This ridiculous plan actually worked marvellously: we 'cooked' the roll-call next morning to conceal his absence and he travelled openly by train to the Swiss border — unfortunately he was nabbed trying to cross, but it nearly came off!

That night the rest of us were standing by to go through our tunnel and beginning to feel very edgy, especially as when the far end was opened up it became apparent that it came out almost exactly under the guard tower. It wasn't the longest ever tunnel but quite long enough, about 30 yards, and so narrow that it was just possible to edge through it prone and using elbows. (Anybody suffering from claustrophobia would be strongly advised to think of some other form of escape.) When I had almost reached the middle with people in front of and behind me there was a hold-up and I lay there unable to move for the best part of half-an-hour with the air getting fouler and fouler. Then we started moving again and eventually it was my turn to emerge, just below that tower. I could hear the sentry above moving around and humming quietly to himself. Very slowly and very quietly I crawled away and got clear.

F/O Peter Wimberley, the author, and F/O 'Bacchus' Baughan at Dulag Luft.

Most of us were working in pairs, though there was the odd loner or two who preferred to go it alone: I was paired off with Peter, a young RAF flying officer. Everybody was working to the same plan, to get to the bridge over the river Main under cover of darkness and cross it before the alarm was raised at morning roll-call, then disperse and hide up the next day. This plan was naturally obvious to the Germans too as soon as they found we had gone, and during the day everybody was rounded up, hiding in the mosquito-ridden damp woods a few miles from the river. Everybody, that is, except Peter and myself!

There is no doubt that Peter and I didn't come from the mould that produces successful escapers. Neither of us spoke any German and we lacked the patience and endurance to lie up all day and only travel by night. In fact we were so inefficient that we were the only two who failed to find the bridge and consequently were on the loose for three days, whereas all the others were back behind bars in the police prison at Frankfurt within 24 hours.

When dawn broke Peter and I found ourselves on the bank of the river some two miles up-stream of the bridge. It was obviously impassable now and we had to make a quick change of plans. We lightly decided that instead of going south to Switzerland we would go north to Schleswig-Holstein, a mere five or six hundred miles distant, and from there find some means of crossing the sea into Sweden. This plan fooled the Germans completely as they concentrated their search south towards Switzerland.

On the first day we plodded north, off the beaten track as much as possible, and got away with it in spite of many curious looks from civilians to whom we had to give a very self-conscious Nazi salute and 'Heil Hitler'. That night we slept hidden in a dew-sodden lush meadow, very cold and huddled together for warmth closer than any two lovers. The second day we plodded on again, north we hoped, and as dusk fell we reckoned we had covered about 20 miles roughly in the direction we wanted to go; so now we only had another 580 or so in front of us. We spent that night in a vast conifer wood, very similar to a Forestry Commission plantation in England. It was intersected by numerous dead straight fire-breaks or rides and every time we stepped into one of these we were visible for miles.

We settled eventually, sleeping fitfully, but were soon disturbed by an uncanny grunting noise and deep breathing. It was pitch dark and one really couldn't even see the proverbial hand in front of one's face. Then something pushed me in the back, and, on being accused, Peter roundly declared that he hadn't touched me. Next Peter accused me of rubbing my feet against his and I in turn indignantly denied having done any such thing. And from time time we could hear heavy breathing and cautious movement all round us; it was most uncanny and we spent a thoroughly restless and unpleasant night. As is usually the case, things that go bump in the night had a simple explanation come daylight. When dawn broke we found that we were surrounded by a large herd of very gentle deer, no doubt as mystified by us as we had been mystified by them!

We continued on our way after sunrise and, finding a beautiful concealed dell overlooking a valley, we stopped to have a rest and to eat some of our rations. It would have been an idyllic spot for a picnic in more happy circumstances and even had a babbling brook nearby. We were much tempted to spend the day there sunbathing but regretfully had to agree that that would hardly further our escape plans. We began to walk along a deserted little country road, then as we approached a corner we suddenly met a herd of pigs being driven by a farm worker. As he got close and I was about to give my famous 'Heil Hitler' he took one look at us and raced off in the opposite direction. We guessed that as we had not been picked up with the others a warning had been passed to look out for us north of the river as well as south; still it was a bit ignominious to be trapped by a swineherd and his pigs. In no time at all we were surrounded by five farmworkers, two with shotguns and the rest with pitchforks, and very menacing they looked. So there we had to remain until 'rescued' by armed police in a car.

After two or three hours in the local village lock-up which was revoltingly filthy, we were transferred to another car with a German officer and guard in it to be driven back to Frankfurt. The officer spoke good English and was sympathetic, having been well treated as a prisoner of the British in the First World War. On the way to Frankfurt he said that if we promised not to try and escape he would stop at a beer garden and we could have some beer and something to eat. Giving parole in such circumstances is, I believe, strictly forbidden; but we gave our word and had some refreshing German beer and apple tart. Back in the cells at the police station we found the rest of our gang and received many congratulations for having lasted so long. A day or two later we were all put on a train and escorted north to *Stalag Luft I* at Lübeck.

Life at *Stalag Luft I* was I guess much the same as in any other PoW camp, but I must tell of an escape attempt with which I was indirectly connected, and which really comes into the 'Billy the Goat' class. Once again I was the camp sports officer responsible for organizing games and exercise. It was mid-winter and there were nine or ten inches of snow on the ground. As at *Dulag Luft* the exercise field was separate from the main compound and it was my job to request the use of it for games from the German Camp Officer. I went to him one day and asked if we could have the field the following afternoon for a game of rugger. Not unnaturally his reply was: 'How can you possibly play football with deep snow on the ground?' At great length I described to him how such conditions were ideal for this type of football played with an oval ball and that the standard of rugger in Scotland was much higher than in England simply because Scotland had so much more snow. I'm afraid I must be a very convincing liar because without much more ado permission was granted for our rugger match next day.

The following afternoon guards were placed round the playing field, the gate was opened and we were counted as we went in; thirty players and one referee. As we started this extraordinary game the guards watched us curiously for the first ten minutes or so, and then deciding we were mad became bored and stamped around trying to keep warm. We had many a long scrum and towards the end of the game one in particular must have lasted the best part of ten minutes. During this time we were busy burying one of our members under the snow. Eventually we started to break up, but immediately scrummed down again — there was a foot sticking out! At last all was well and the game ended successfully. We trooped back through the gate, being counted once more, but by pushing and shoving somebody was able to stumble and fall after being counted, crawl back and get counted again; thus the numbers coming out tallied with the numbers going in. How the Germans failed to spot this awful snow mound, with a wisp of steam rising from it, in the middle of the field is incredible. And how our fellow managed to lie absolutely still in intense cold until dark is also incredible. That night he cut his way through the wire and was away, only to be picked up in the countryside two or three days later.

Life in camp continued, boring most of the time, but enlivened occasionally by some incredibly funny (and risky) happenings that gave us a good laugh and not unnaturally infuriated the Germans: indeed there were times when I could almost have felt sorry for them. There was one fellow who disguised himself as an Alsatian dog: he was going quite well towards the wire one dark night until he had the misfortune to meet a real Alsatian who wasn't fooled for a moment!

Then there was the time when somebody discovered a microphone behind a fire-place brick in our assembly room; we were being bugged. We left it there a week or two cheerfully passing over some useful misinformation, but finally decided that the risk of somebody actually passing genuine information was too great and that the 'mike' would have to go. Its leads were therefore connected to the electric light circuit and the switch made. We had delightful visions of somebody in the German *Kommandantur* sitting listening in and suddenly having his ears, or perhaps even his head, blown off. For a quarter of an hour nothing happened then, marching towards the camp main gate, and headed by the German Commandant himself, was a small army with sub-machine guns at the ready. All the prisoners were fallen in and the Senior British Officer was accused by an infuriated Commandant of sabotaging electrical circuits in the camp. His reply was, 'What circuits Herr Commandant? The electric light appears to be in full working order.' This put the Commandant in rather a spot, but he was so angry that he admitted it was a listening device circuit. I can still remember our SBO's bland and 'surprised' reply: 'But surely, Herr Commandant, microphones in PoW quarters are not permitted by the Geneva Convention?' Eventually we were allowed to fall out and the Germans took revenge on us by stopping our Red Cross parcels for a month and pretending that communications with Switzerland and Sweden had broken down. As we got a little leaner and hungrier during that month we could still chuckle over this incident and were always on the look-out for a German without ears!

Each evening at this camp we were barred and locked into our respective barrack blocks, and, in theory only, we were not supposed to be able to get out. At lock-up a detail of six German soldiers under the command of an NCO used to march into the

View from the compound, Stalag Luft III, Sagan.

compound to do the locking up. They always marched in in file, would lock the doors and slam great shutters tight over the windows. When they had finished they would fall in in two ranks, right turn, and march out again. We accompanied their arrival and departure by whistling 'It's off to work we go ...' from Walt Disney's *Snow White and the Seven Dwarfs*. This used to make a few smile and a lot very angry.

One night they had completed their locking up and fallen in in two ranks in front of their NCO, but instead of there being six men there were eight. The extra were two of our officers, wonderfully disguised in home-made German uniforms and with wooden rifles. The German NCO gave the order: 'Right Turn, Quick March' and out they marched through the main gate and sentries, to be halted in front of the guardroom in the outer camp. Here the NCO stood them at ease and went into the guardroom to report all correct to the guard commander. Now he should have come out almost immediately, dismissed his detail, and our two escapers would have drifted away into the darkness. Unfortunately he was rather a long time and the German next to one of our chaps started chatting. Had he been a really fluent German speaker they might have got away with it, but as his answer to all questions was 'Ya' or 'Nein', in a very poor accent, suspicions were aroused and they were both bundled into the guardroom!

I remained at *Stalag Luft I* for about a year before we were all moved to *Stalag Luft III*, a new camp for flying PoWs which had been built at Sagan, a small town about 80 or 90 miles north-west of Breslau. This camp was roughly in the middle of Germany and discouragingly remote from any neutral border, not that this deterred the confirmed escapers. I don't think there was ever a moment when there was not at least one tunnel under construction. It was from this camp that the 'Wooden Horse' escape and the 'Great Escape' took place. After a year there the camp was becoming overcrowded and the German authorities decided that another compound to hold about 1000 prisoners would have to be built. Until it was completed they had to move several hundred of us to a camp in Poland near Posen. The Germans detailed those who were to move, but at the same time agreed to take any who volunteered to go.

Once again, against all my principles, I volunteered and found myself in *Offlag* (Officers Camp) *XXI B*, about 160 miles from Berlin and some 60 miles from the German-Polish border. This voluntary move on my part turned out to be a great mistake. The camp was bare and spartan, over a hundred men to each barrack but with no sub-divisions into rooms and the winter climate was particularly cruel. The German Commandant was a rather eccentric disciplinarian who was quite confident that nobody was going to escape from his camp! He was an ex-engineer officer, what we call a sapper, and had had the brilliant idea of surrounding the camp with buried land mines which, he informed us, would be detonated at unspecified intervals so that anybody tunnelling near them would undoubtedly be killed. This was no idle bluff: we could be sitting reading peacefully when we would suddenly be startled out of our wits by a shattering explosion just outside the perimeter wire. It took us only a few weeks to locate all his mines: some we neutralized and those we couldn't we avoided. I think that during the year we were there we had three successful tunnels through which quite a number escaped though I can't remember any

Lt Cdrs James Buckley and John Casson at Stalag Luft III

getting back to England or to a neutral country. In fact a very great friend of mine, a Lieutenant-Commander RN reached the north German coast successfully, only to be drowned trying to cross over to Sweden by canoe.

After a year at *Offlag XXI B* we were returned to the newly built compound at *Stalag Luft III*. Following our rather rigorous year in Poland this seemed relatively luxurious and we soon settled down to the sort of PoW life we had become accustomed to. The tunnelling and escape attempts continued unabated. It was from this compound that the long and wonderfully constructed tunnel was successfully completed for the 'Great Escape'. The plan was to push over a hundred prisoners out through this tunnel at one go, a plan of which I strongly disapproved and I refused to take the place offered to me. It was now 1944, the Russians were advancing, and Hitler appeared to be madder and more unpredictable than ever. I told the Senior British Officer that a mass escape would result in reprisals out of all proportion to the mere handful who might complete the escape successfully; we all knew that most would be recaptured within a few days. I wanted the tunnel to be used to slip two or three of our chaps out at intervals; in this way there would be no country-wide hue and cry, we could cook the roll-calls and give them a good start, and the Germans need not necessarily discover the tunnel as a small number of escapers could have been got out over or through the wire. As it turned out between 70 and 80 went out through this tunnel and all were recaptured within a week save two. Then came the reprisals. Hitler immediately ordered that all the recaptured prisoners were to be shot. He was eventually persuaded to reduce this to fifty, and fifty of our British PoWs were murdered by the Gestapo. The climate at that time in Germany was certainly not suited to mass escapes.

I can never remember a time whilst I was a PoW when we did not get the BBC Radio News by means of an illicit and very well concealed wireless receiving set. In the winter of 1944 we were all following the Russian advance on the Eastern Front with the greatest of interest; they really were beginning to get quite close to our camp. One day we were warned by the Germans to be ready to leave and we were allowed to prepare home-made rucksacks for such possessions as we could carry. A few evenings later, at about 0200 hours on a bitterly cold but fine night, we marched out.

We were on the march for two days and one night. I shall never forget that night which was spent in a huge barn with a broken roof. The floor was covered with ice and we were packed so close that those lying in the middle had to stay put regardless of anything they might wish or have to do. Towards the end of the second day we arrived at a railway marshalling yard and were herded into closed cattle trucks. In previous more peaceful days in France I had always been amused by these trucks with the words *8 chevaux, 40 hommes* on the side. Well in my truck we were *50 hommes* and pretty crowded and unpleasant it was; especially when the train halted during an air raid and we, locked and barred in, were a particularly captive target. We had two days in this confounded train followed by quite a short march to a *Marlag*, a camp for naval PoWs, not far from Bremerhaven. Here we were given a cursory search, though even this took hours, then shepherded into a compound of our own and kept separate from the naval prisoners with whom, unknown to the Germans, we soon managed to set up efficient communications. We were very crowded and missed many of our prized possessions which we had been unable to carry on the march, but at least the Red Cross parcels were still coming through so we didn't go too hungry.

The months at this *Marine Lager* passed much the same as months do in any PoW camp until April 1945 when the Germans were threatened by the advance of the British and Americans from the west. At this stage of a war PoWs become very valuable bargaining hostages for the threatened side, of course, and once again we were marched out and away from our potential liberators. This time we really were a vast column with naval and RAF prisoners combined and we drove the German guards frantic by going as slowly as possible so that our own forces might catch up with us. We were on the march for a week or ten days, always heading north towards Schleswig-Holstein. Fortunately it was brilliant, warm spring weather and I really enjoyed the freedom and wide open spaces. We slept everywhere, in open fields, in barns, in haystacks and farm buildings of every sort. In general the local populace was co-operative, at times friendly, and always apprehensive. By now the outcome of the war was obvious and the ambition of all Germans was to be captured or occupied by the British and Americans rather than the Russians. There was only one occasion on this march when I was glad of our German guards and that was when we were marching, or rather straggling, through the outskirts of Hamburg. Hamburg had been very, very heavily bombed so when the local people found out that we were flying PoWs they became extremely hostile, and without our armed guards there might have been some ugly incidents.

I and most of those who had been in my compound at *Stalag Luft III* ended up eventually in a large farm somewhere well inside Schleswig-Holstein. It appeared to be a model farm and owed its well-kept and neat appearance to the ample forced labour employed there. We settled down in the numerous out-buildings very comfortably and after a day or so noticed that our guards had melted away, and from that moment roles were reversed. German officers and all ranks started to drift into 'our' farm to surrender and I was given the job of supervising their disarming and placing them in a large barn which we set aside for our prisoners. Apart from one or two fanatical Nazis who were still 'Heil Hitlering' all over the place they were a cowed and dejected lot and appeared relieved to have become prisoners of the British. They caused no trouble.

Avro Lancaster of 635 Squadron RAF employed on Operation Exodus, the repatriation of PoWs. Each Lancaster could cram up to 25 passengers aboard for the two hour flight back to Blighty.

14

The prisoner returns

From then on things moved quickly and my memories of them tend to be a little vague. It was on, I think, the 5th or 6th of May that the German prisoners started coming in in increasing numbers. Though we did not know it VE Day was just around the corner and we remained 'incommunicado' until the afternoon of 6th May when a British scout car roared into our farm camp and our position was radioed back to the nearest HQ. The next day a large convoy of lorries arrived and we were driven for hours back across Germany towards the west. I can remember being very hospitably entertained that night in the temporary Officers Mess of a local unit and the following day I managed to hitch a lift back to England in a Lancaster which landed at Wing Aerodrome in Bucks. I can clearly remember the thrill and great surge of nostalgia I felt when the Lancaster's pilot told us, 'We are

now crossing the coast of England'. From Wing we were sent on that day to London by train where we spent the night in some sort of Officer's Hostel, and then, even at this stage of the war, service red tape enmeshed me.

All RM officers were based on one of three HQs, Plymouth, Portsmouth or Chatham. I was a Plymouth Marine and in spite of the fact that I lived at Worthing, only 1¼ hours train ride from London, the powers-that-be insisted that I report immediately to the RM barracks at Plymouth. And so I was issued with a railway warrant from Paddington to Plymouth and set off on the long journey to the west country and away from home. I arrived at Plymouth station about 1800 hours in the evening, rang up the barracks for transport and found myself outside the Officers Mess at 1845 to find a cocktail party in progress. Now I was still dressed in the tattered and filthy battledress I had been wearing for our final two weeks march across Germany and looked a very curious object. I know I had been viewed with some suspicion on the train down and had to keep on making explanations.

As I hesitated outside the Mess door I could hear sounds of chatter and laughter, including female chatter and laughter. The latter made me even more hesitant to enter; I hadn't seen or spoken to a girl for five years, but I couldn't stand there for ever and eventually had to push open the door and enter. I was instantly spotted and a hush fell over the party, everyone gazing at this extraordinary apparition; it was excruciatingly embarrassing! Then, of course, after explanations I was right royally, too royally, accepted and entertained, being plied with food and drink that my poor old contracted stomach really couldn't cope with. Fortunately the Principal Medical Officer came in, sized up the situation and put an immediate stop to my feasting. Even so the next day I had a terribly upset stomach and couldn't do justice to any of the food we had dreamt about so much as PoWs. I was then taken away and given a new battledress plus a complete change of clothing, and put to bed. After a medical check the following morning I was sent on three months leave on double rations.

I have often been asked whether my time as a PoW wasn't just five wasted years of my life. To some it must seem so but I am not convinced that any period of one's life can be written off as wasted. Looking back on it after all these years I can't help feeling that it taught me a lot. It certainly taught me to appreciate the basic necessities of life that we all take for granted — enough food and the freedom to come and go as you will are just two of them. And we were all certainly taught a great lesson in toleration. You cannot live cheek by jowl with others not of your own choosing, year after year, in harmony without being tolerant. Rather than there being a lot of squabbling, or even fighting, a remarkable number of good and lasting friendships were made. We had our disagreements of course, but they were seldom serious.

One of the most disturbing aspects of being taken PoW is that your sentence is indeterminate. If you are given a sentence of three, five, or even more years at least you have a date or goal to look forward to. But being taken prisoner in the early days of the war, as I was, when could you expect to be released? And would it be on the winning or defeated side? With France about to fall and the isolation of Great Britain imminent I was under no illusions that I was going to be a short-term prisoner, and so it was during my first year that I made myself a calendar on which I could cross off the days, just as I used to do at the start of a term at boarding school. When I tell you that my prison calendar was made out for four years you can see that it wasn't long enough by almost a year. I remember a newly captured American pilot coming into my room at Sagan and, seeing my calendar on which I had crossed off the days for over three and a half years, exclaim 'Gee, I'll never last that long!', to which I rather flippantly replied, 'You'll make it chum, the first two years are the worst, then you'll find you're settling down!' When my four year calendar expired I didn't make another, the end of the war seemed to be approaching by then.

It was interesting to see how different people adjusted to the restricted and unnatural life of a prisoner of war, a life remote and alien to what should have been one's normal existence. There were no decisions to make, no risks which had to be taken, and at times it seemed that life was completely without aim. Some just drifted from day to day, year after year, almost completely institutionalized. Some found an occupation that helped to pass the time more or less usefully; tunnel digging, music, languages, acting, helping to administer the running of the camp, forging escape documents, teaching or just endlessly planning to escape. Two examples stand out in my mind. The first was a naval officer who specialized in escape tunnels. As soon as one was finished or discovered he would organize another. He was the 'tunnel king', but as far as I know he never went out through one. The second was a young Australian flying officer who apparently could find no occupation and couldn't adjust to his new situation: month after month he deteriorated in spite of all efforts to help him. One day in broad daylight he made a dash for the barbed wire — the machine guns chattered and he slumped dead across the top of the perimeter wire. As we buried him with full military honours I couldn't help thinking of the waste of a charming young man who had survived being shot down and taken prisoner, only to become so disturbed mentally that he took an action amounting to suicide.

I managed to survive my five years reasonably well, though I did have my moments of acute depression and frustration like most others. To keep myself occupied I volunteered firstly as camp sports officer and later as camp clothing officer, responsible for the distribution of Red Cross and other clothing, especially to newly arrived prisoners who came just with the clothes they stood up in. I also became 'Cook of the Mess' for the six of us in my room. This took up a lot of my time and ingenuity and I became expert at making up meals from the food in Red Cross parcels and the few rations issued by the Germans. The equal division of these meals was absolutely vital; more serious rows and arguments arose when someone thought they were not getting their fair share than from any other reason. Hunger could bring out some very basic and unpleasant instincts. I overcame this problem in my Mess by first dividing the food for any one meal into six equal portions (or as equal as it was possible to make them): then, from a shuffled and cut pack one card was dealt to each portion, the portion with the lowest card going to the youngest officer, the highest to the eldest, and so on in between! There were still moans of course, but if someone felt he had got the smallest helping he could only fairly attribute it to the luck of the draw and not to someone else's low cunning.

Apart from sports officer, clothing officer and 'Cook of the Mess', I did have one other job not quite of my own choosing and with possibilities I found it wise not to dwell on too deeply. Soon after the 'Great Escape' in which fifty recaptured prisoners were murdered on Hitler's orders, the Russian advance from the east was speeding up and our Senior British Officer had to consider the possibility that a mad Hitler might well order the liquidation of all British flying PoWs. This possibility was discussed in conference, and the real dangers recognized and accepted. When we had learned of the murder of our fellow officers after their recapture, the German authorities had had a hundred or so NCOs armed with sub-machine guns standing by to rush into our compound in case we rioted. There had of course been no intention to riot though relations between captor and captive became remarkably hostile for a time. It was not thought likely that any drastic action would be carried out by the existing German authorities at the camp, who had by and large acted corrctly under International Law and the Geneva Convention. The danger lay in the oft-repeated threat that if we continued to escape the administration of our camp would be handed over to the SS, and it was most unlikely that they would recognize International Law or Geneva Convention if ordered by Hitler to eliminate us in the face of the Russian advance. The conference decided that if elimination or shipping off to concentration camps appeared imminent we were not going to submit tamely as so many of the tragic Jewish victims had done. Consequently the Klim Club was formed. Klim (milk spelt backwards) was the excellent powdered milk that came in Canadian Red Cross food parcels and was chosen as the code name for a party of about forty men who, if the need arose, were to storm two or three of the watch towers in an attempt to get the machine guns and rifles. It was realized that these were desperate measures, that casualties would be very high (perhaps even 100%) but that in the face of such a situation there was no alternative. Those who volunteered and were accepted for the Klim Club were all skilled in unarmed combat and knowledgeable about German small arms. I was asked to command this gang of desperadoes and the fact that I am writing this now is probably sufficient for readers to guess that we were never called into action!

My five years is long since over, but you will see from what I have written that one tends to remember chiefly what was humorous or exciting while the endless humdrum, boring, sordid and pointless days tend to be forgotten. That is, I think, nature's way of helping in life. As the only surviving officer of my 1940 squadron perhaps I should be grateful that I was taken prisoner so early on, for had I not been, my chances of surviving another five years of war must have been very small indeed.

This story set out to be a short account of one man's very brief war, mostly in Norway, and as a prisoner of war, and should end here; and but for a telephone call out of the blue thirty years after the war ended it would have done. This phone call united me once again with Skua L2940 which I had crash-landed on the frozen lake up in the snowy, rugged heights of Norway at Grotli. To lead up to this extraordinary event and for the sake of continuity I must sketch in briefly what happened in the intervening years.

15

My Service career ends

After my three months leave I was posted to RNAS Lee-on-Solent for a flying refresher course. I think flying is rather like riding a bicycle in that once you have learnt you never forget. Even after an interval of over five years I had no difficulty in flying again, despite the fact that during this refresher course I was flying Harvards, Avengers, Fireflies, Barracudas and Seafires, aircraft I had never even seen before, let alone flown. I enjoyed the course immensely and had no difficulty in qualifying.

On 10th November 1945 I was appointed Commander (Flying) and Officer in Charge of RNAS Lee-on-Solent. This was a difficult command and looking back on it, not really suited to someone who had recently completed five years as a PoW. My Navy was still in the early days of the war and I had had no chance to get acclimatized to the great changes that so many war years had imposed on the Services; changes of custom, discipline, outlook, aircraft and a host of other things. In addition it was an awkward command as Lee-on-Solent contained not only the airfield and its flying, but also the Fleet Air Arm barracks housing great numbers of officers and ratings who had nothing to do with the actual flying side. The whole station was under the command of a Commodore RN and the extent of the authority of the Officer in Charge of the flying station (under the Commodore) was not well defined. I like to think I coped quite well, but must confess that I was never very happy in this posting and found at times that my responsibilities lay very heavy on me. Fortunately the Commodore was a man of perception, of great ability and experience, and of great charm. After six months he sent for me and said that he suspected that I was not very happy in my work, though he was generous enough to add that he had no complaints as to the way I had been carrying it out. He added that he liked his officers to feel that they could enjoy their work and that he would be glad to endorse my request for a change if I wished to make one. I have never been able to decide whether or not this was a kind way of giving me the 'sack', but at the time I gratefully accepted his suggestion.

After handing over my command I found myself appointed to number 14 Course at the Empire Central Flying School at RAF Hullavington. This was an extremely advanced course for experienced pilots, ranging from Flight Lieutenant to Wing Commander, drawn from all over the Commonwealth, and sometimes from

EMPIRE CENTRAL FLYING SCHOOL
Royal Air Force

This is to Certify that

Capt R J Partridge DSO

of the **Royal Marines**

has successfully graduated from the

Empire Central Flying School.

No 14   Course 1946

Date 9th November

[signature]

Air Commodore
Commandant ECFS.

Roderic Hill

Air Marshal
Air Member for Training.

America as well. They liked to have as varied a pupil population as possible, and never having had a Marine officer before were glad to include me for that reason. The flying was on various types of aircraft and I found myself having to fly twin-engined Bristol Buckmasters, four-engined Avro Lancasters, a Hotspur glider and even the twin-engined Gloster Meteor jet. Having been a single-engined fighter pilot all my flying life this was quite an experience and challenge to me, and it was with great surprise and relief that at the end of the course I learnt that I had graduated with a Distinguished Pass. I was also paid the great compliment of being asked to remain there as a tutor. Well, flying all these strange aircraft was one thing, but teaching other experienced pilots to fly them was different, and I declined the offer and accepted instead a posting to the Directorate of Air Organization and Training in the Admiralty.

I feel I should add in passing that during this very intensive course at Hullavington I also got married! Leave during the course was strictly discouraged but I managed to get a short break on a Bank Holiday week-end. We were married on the Saturday morning, had Sunday and Monday for our honeymoon, and at 0900 hours on Tuesday morning I was due to carry out my first solo in a jet aircraft, the Gloster Meteor. I'm glad to say that all went well, both the honeymoon and the solo, and we are still most happily married, my kindergarten girl-friend and I!

The usual tour of duty at the Admiralty was two years, but I managed to spend three years there. I was living with my wife at Angmering village in West Sussex and commuted to London daily from Arundel station. Hence I had the best of both worlds, a home life and a service life which I found most satisfying and enjoyable. Under my director, a Captain RN, I was responsible for flying training in the Fleet Air Arm and I found the advanced course I had completed at RAF Hullavington of great value. However at the end of three years it was obvious that I couldn't stay for ever and there was a big question mark over my service future. I had been flying or connected with flying for seventeen years, since 1933, and was completely out of touch with my own Corps, the Royal Marines, to which I really should now return. I had been promoted to Major a couple of years previously but didn't fancy my chances of further promotion very highly as a Marine officer. I was then given the chance of turning over to the Navy as a Commander (Air), but felt that at the age of forty it was a bit late in life to change Service. By length of service I had just qualified for a pension and, after talking it over with my wife, decided to 'retire at my own request'. This was granted and marks the end of my service career.

What to do next was the question. It was 1950, the post-war period of rationing and shortages was still in full swing, and there were many, many others like me trying to fit themselves back into civilian life. By this time we had a son and a daughter, aged three and two, and we both craved the peace and quiet of the countryside. Accordingly we bought a small farm of 100 acres at Cross-in-Hand in East Sussex. We knew very little about farming and for the first year or two I had to employ a bailiff. From the start I was determined to master all the farming arts required on this, a dairy farm, and it wasn't too long before I could go solo in everything and was quite capable of doing any of the jobs my staff had to do. At the end of the second year I was able to do without a bailiff and took full command myself. A farm is a marvellous place on which to bring up a young family, and we

The family growing up, Dudsland Farm, East Sussex, 1953.

worked it for the best part of eleven years, building up a fine pedigree herd of Jersey cows and latterly also a 2000 flock of poultry producing hatching eggs for the broiler industry.

There were of course crises from time to time, there always are when you have a hundred head of valuable cattle to deal with, but we coped and became more and more efficient as the years passed. Never in my life before had I worked so hard physically or led a healthier life. Like most small farmers we were always short of capital and I suppose in a way over-staffed. The trouble was that we liked a tidy well kept place and a nicely groomed herd; but neat hedges, clean ditches and sleek cattle are labour-absorbing without bringing in any revenue. The result was that the milking herd seldom did any better than just break even financially, but the poultry flock was a very different matter. Two thousand hens and their attendant cockerels were managed by one girl during the week and myself at the weekends. It was at the height of the broiler boom and when we were picking up 10,000 eggs a week the return for so small a labour force was excellent. I also found poultry keeping on this scale most interesting.

Our children were now in their teens and would obviously soon be leaving home and I was just on the wrong side of fifty and finding the physical work getting a little harder. We decided therefore, regretfully, to sell the farm, buy a small country house with a few acres and continue with poultry only. We bought a very old and very beautiful house with about six acres but before we could get the poultry organized the broiler market began to look less certain and before committing considerable capital to creating our new flock we decided to wait and see how the market developed. We are still waiting fifteen years later!

16

Full circle

By now of course the war, Skuas, Norway and PoW camps were all nothing more than a dim memory and we seldom thought or talked of them. Then one summer day in 1974 an unexpected telephone call brought all those memories crowding back on top of us once more.

This telephone call came from the Royal Naval Air Station at Yeovilton, the home of the Flag Officer commanding the Fleet Air Arm and also of the Fleet Air Arm Museum. I was asked on the 'phone if I was the pilot who had crash-landed a Skua on a frozen lake in the Norwegian mountains in 1940. When I replied 'Yes', I was asked if I could give the number of the aircraft and I said that if they could hang on and if I could find my flying log book I would let them know. My log book, I knew, was somewhere in the house which, with us, usually means several weeks search! Surprisingly this time I found it in the bottom drawer of my desk within a minute or two and was able to pick up the 'phone and say that it was Skua L2940. There was a great cry of triumph from the other end and it was explained to me that my aircraft had been discovered at the bottom of the lake by a Norwegian sub-aqua diving club, and that it appeared to be in remarkably good condition. As it was the only Skua left in the world, plans were being made to recover it and bring it back to the Fleet Air Arm Museum at Yeovilton.

Up to this time I had seldom spoken of my brief war experiences, even to my family; I was happy to forget about it all and had firmly refused to be included in any books of war incidents. There was one occasion when I broke this rule and that was in 1946 or 1947 when there was a knock on the door of our home at Angmering. On the doorstep were two very pleasant and persuasive reporters from the BBC who explained that they were doing a story for BBC Radio about war incidents to be entitled 'Now it can be told'. I asked them in and we chatted about the programme they were doing and I said I was sorry but there was no question of my going to BBC London for a recording. They were obviously prepared for this reply saying that all I had to do was to sit back in my armchair and tell my story into a microphone which they would bring into the house on a long lead from their car. As they had gone to all the trouble of finding me at my rather remote home it seemed churlish to refuse and I was trapped. When the programme finally went on the air I got a cheque for £15 for the first broadcast, £10 for the repeat, £5 for a final repeat and then dropped into obscurity again.

The finding and identifying of Skua L2940 and its pilot was really going to disturb my quiet country retirement and there didn't seem to be any way in which I could gracefully avoid it. Not only were the Fleet Air Arm preparing to recover the aircraft for their marvellous museum but a film company, Charterhall Films Ltd, were also planning, in co-operation with the Navy, to make a documentary of it in which I would be asked to narrate on location the happenings on that long forgotten and long past day 27th April 1940.

Things really started with a press release from the Navy and a meeting at RNAS Lee-on-Solent of the leaders of the recovery expedition, representatives of the film company, myself and of course the press. It was really hectic and I had to face innumerable interviews and photographers which resulted in accounts of my story in both the local and national press, none of which were really accurate as is so often the case, and sometimes with embarrassing headlines such as 'Wartime hero re-united with his aircraft after 34 years'!

The film company wanted me to go for a week to Grotli whilst they filmed the recovery of the aircraft and I told my story. I was most unwilling and had grave doubts of my being able to perform adequately in front of cameras and micro-phones, but I was eventually persuaded by my wife and daughter, and one day in July 1974 found myself on an aircraft bound for Oslo. There we changed planes and set off again for Alesund, where we were met by a minibus and had a long drive up into the mountains to Grotli. I remembered quite clearly how much the Norwegian scenery had impressed me during those rather desperate war days, but seeing it again under such different circumstances I could only marvel once more at its breathtaking beauty and grandeur. I could admire it at leisure with no fear of being bombed, shot at or taken prisoner. I have never regretted my return.

We arrived at Grotli late in the evening but it was still light. It really was an extra-ordinary feeling; if you had dropped me there blindfolded, then suddenly removed the blindfold, I would instantly have recognized every feature. There was the lake where we had crash-landed; there was the hut we had sheltered in and had our meal of porridge; there was the outhouse where I had found my old pair of skis; and there was the Grotli hotel, now much enlarged, but the original part just the same. Nothing had really changed except that this time it was July not April, and all the snow had gone. I was right royally welcomed by the hotel family who told me that their father, Sevald Grotli, was alive and still living in the little farmhouse that had acted as headquarters for the ski patrols all those years ago. They said that he hadn't been very well, being now over 70, and that they had been trying to persuade him to move down into the valley. He refused however, saying that he had lived in the mountains all his life and that if he had to die it would be there and nowhere else. I was to meet him next day.

After a lovely Norwegian breakfast the following morning I was told that I would not be needed until the evening when they would be filming 'The Reunion of Partridge and Grotli' at his house. I asked if it would be possible to have some sort of rehearsal but was told that all I had to do was to act naturally, and for all my filming I really received little direction other than this; not an easy thing to do if you are not a professional actor and have never been in front of a cine camera before. So I met Sevald Grotli again that evening in his little farmhouse parlour, now full of

wires, microphones, cameras and all the paraphernalia of film making. He had also been told to act naturally and was perhaps more embarrassed than I. They had to cut most of that scene but what remained wasn't too bad, though I guess I'm never going to make a film star. It was a moving experience to meet the old fellow again and I think he was pleased to see me. He had kept my flying clothing and a few possessions I had left behind there all those years ago and was filmed returning them to me. This scene really turned out quite well. He was now a fine, craggy, 'old man of the mountains' and still well in command of all those around him. It was with genuine regret and a sense of loss that when I came down to breakfast next day I found his daughter in tears and she told me that her father had been found dead early that morning. Sevald Grotli had died of a heart attack up in the mountains not even the Germans could make him leave.

The filming was divided into two parts, one for the actual recovery of the aircraft including many underwater shots; and the other recording my narration of the story at the lake, the hut and the hotel. There was also one scene featuring me examining the wreckage of the Heinkel which had crash-landed on a small lake only a few miles from mine. It was an eerie experience wandering among those scattered remains and I could not help wondering why he had chosen this little lake instead of the larger one, and what would have happened if we had both landed on the same lake. Would we have continued the battle on land or would we have called a truce? I also had visions of the bullet-riddled body of the Heinkel rear-gunner abandoned with the wrecked aircraft as the three survivors started to struggle through the snow to safety in the same way as we had done. I had been told that his body had eventually been buried with full military honours by the advancing Germans and I found his grave quite close to the hotel.

Remains of the Heinkel bomber and one of its engines (opposite), all apparently well preserved.

My part in the film was finished in a week and I had to return to England before the recovery of the aircraft had been completed. Before I left however I did get a good view of it raised to within fifteen feet of the surface and I marvelled at how well these pure mountain waters had preserved it for 34 years. The only damage had been done by the fire which had completely destroyed the cockpit sections; but the engine, mainplanes and empennage (tail unit) appeared to be in a wonderful state of preservation. These remains now lie in the Fleet Air Arm Museum at RNAS Yeovilton and really make quite an impressive exhibit of the only Blackburn Skua left in the world.

Whilst all this filming and recovery went on the Norwegian press descended on Grotli in hordes; they arrived by motor coach, by car and even by floatplane, landing on the lake. It is no exaggeration to say that for several days the Skua story was front page news in every Norwegian paper. I mention this because it was this publicity that brought about some very interesting and unexpected sequels. The first was a marvellous letter from a Norwegian, Reidar Hov, and I feel I can do no better than to quote this as I received it.

Major R.T. Partridge.

Dear Sir.

Let me first tell you that a reporting in the Norwegian newspaper 'Aftenposten' is the direct cause for my writing to you. I am aiming at a reporting last summer with this heading: Silent Briton relives airfights. A journalist from the newspaper had met you at Grotli, where you stayed to assist by the rescue of the plain in which you were shot down during the war in Norway in April 1940. In the interview was also told that you were shot down another time, and this time over the Trondheimfjord area, and shortly afterwards you were taken prisoner by the Germans. This occurred on June 13. 1940.

I could hardly believe my own eyes when I read this — there was no doubt about it any longer: This was the very same pilot I had met just the same day his plane was shot down over the Trondheimfjord, and he himself was taken prisoner. Thus he had yet survived the war and the captivity!

May I allow myself more detailed to go back to the summer 1940. I stayed then on the very same place in the Trondheimfjord area where this happened. Early in the morning on June 13. I was waked by the shooting from an airfight that was going on right over our heads. The result of the fight was that one of the two fighting planes was hit and caught fire, and I could see how the damaged plane rushed like a burning torch direct in the sea, while a black parachute went slowly down towards the fjord.

Some hours later I had a phonecall from the neighbouring farm saying that an injured English pilot was brought there. Two fishermen had picked him up and brought him there in a rowboat, because they thought that the Germans had not yet arrived at this place. The people of the farm (the name of the farm is *Stallvik*) had called me because they knew I had some knowledge of English. Of course I willingly did as they told me.

When I arrived at the farm you had just come from the doctors and had been dressed because of injures you had got. I can still remember many of the questions you asked during our conversation, and which I tried to answer.

I can't help mentioning the deep impression you made upon me because of the calmness and selfcontrol you showed in spite of the serious situation you were in. Later I got to know that in the afternoon on the same day the Germans had traced you, and you were taken prisoner.

This was in short what occurred on June 13. 1940. Later during the war I and the people on the farm to which you were brought, many times reminded each other of 'the English pilot', and we wondered what had happened him later.

34 years were to pass before I accidentally came across the reporting/interview in the newspaper. So strange can things be!

Usually I spend my holidays on the same place in the Trondheimfjord area, and on the farm where I met you in 1940, many of those who witnessed this, are still alive. When I last summer told them what the newspaper had written about you and your fate, it arose a kind of sensation. But let me add: An absolutely joyful sensation!

If you should be of the opinion that I should not have written to you, but rather have saved you from reminding you of things you would rather forget, I beg your pardon. May I say as an excuse that I do not write to remind you of bad things in the past, but just to express the joy it was to experience that you had survived the years of the war.

I know that this joy is shared by 'the people at the Trondheimfjord' who recall what happened at that time. They too have asked me to write to you, and on behalf of all those 'who remember' I ask you to receive our heartiest greetings and best wishes. Of several causes the writing has been postponed until now.

I should think it is unnecessary to say that it would be a pleasure for all of us to hear from you. May be some time you will come back to Norway?

Yours sincerely
Reidar Hov.
P.S. I have not succeeded in getting your address, but The British Embassy in Oslo has been so kind to help me to get it.

At last: Excuse me for my imperfect English!
R.H.

Reidar Hov and I have been writing to each other at intervals since I received this first letter and I am hoping one of these days to join him at Stallvik Farm on Trondheimfjord. Regretfully I have learned from him that one of the fishermen was drowned some years ago and that the other died comparatively recently.

The second sequel was to me even more astonishing and again started with a letter. Before and during the filming in Norway the producer had made exhaustive efforts to trace the pilot of the Heinkel, but without success. Obviously his film was going to be that much better if he could have both the English and the German pilot telling their stories on location. But when the film was completed, the aircraft recovered and back in England and the dust, so to speak, of the whole affair had settled I received another letter. It was postmarked München, Germany, and was from Horst Schopis, the pilot of the Heinkel!

25 Oktober 1975

Dear Mr. Partridge!
Some months ago Mr. Cliff Vincent from Bristol wrote a letter to me. He asked for details about the war in Norway. By this way we came into correspondence. I asked him if it would be possible for him to find out the name and Adress of my last counterpart in the air battle nearby Andalsnes, April 1940. He asked the Ministry of Defence and I got the answer in July: 'The *meeting* has been well documented. The Skua was flown by Captain RT Partridge! He is still alive!' But not a word about your adress!

At the same time, an old friend of me, the former Cpt. Steinbach, who was shot down on the same place, at the same day, now living in Hamburg, a Dipl. Ing. at the 'British Petrol' sent me the 'BP-Shield May 1975' with the 'Operation Skua-Story' in it. There I could read: 'Partridge is now a farmer in Sussex!' To find out the rest of your adress was not too difficult for Cliff Vincent!

Dear Mr. Partridge, we met together 35 years ago, rearly under other circumstances. Still in a British prison-camp I found in a newspaper your article 'Shot down Nazis, met them ashore', and now the Skua story! I think it could be very interesting for us to have another meeting under better conditions! I wrote to Cliff V. 'From my point of view we never have been ennemies, we were *counterparts!*' I would like to met you again, to look into your eyes again, to shake your hands! I hope we can get friends!

My wife and I, we invite you with your wife very kindly to visit us in Munchen. But if it is impossible for you to come to Germany, we can manage to come for a visit to Britain.

I hope to hear from you very soon.

Yours sincearly

Horst Schopis

I was delighted to get it and replied immediately, and we corresponded fairly regularly thereafter until one day he wrote that he and his wife were flying to London for a 'winter-break' package weekend holiday and could I and my wife meet them in London for a meal. I replied that we would both be delighted to meet them but suggested that it would be much nicer if, on the Saturday of their weekend, they could catch a train from Victoria to Haywards Heath where I would meet them and drive them to my home for lunch. This was agreed and with some trepidation I found myself standing on the platform at Haywards Heath station waiting to meet a German I had only seen briefly 34 years ago in what can best be described as very

The author, his wife Fay and Horst Schopis during the visit in 1977

unusual circumstances. I must confess to being nervous. Would we like each other? Would we understand each other? Would we even recognize each other?

Soon I saw the long London train approaching and with a hiss of air brakes and a slowing rumble it came to a stop. By some good fortune it happened that out of the compartment opposite to where I stood stepped a tall distinguished figure wearing what I call a Tyrolean hat. He looked up, our eyes met, and we instantly recognized each other. It was a good meeting with some emotion and a lot of feeling on both sides. I was introduced to his very charming and attractive wife, and as her English was fluent and Horst's was adequate there were no problems of communication. I would add here that my German, even after five years as a PoW, is extremely limited and it was a great relief not to have to try and use it.

Our lunch party and whole meeting were an unqualified success. Here were we two chatting away happily together and both liking each other, whereas the first time we met we were doing our utmost to kill each other. We all agreed that in the civilized world there should be, must be agreement that international disputes are settled round the conference table and not by war. But then Horst and I both claimed that we were not pacifists and would fight again to defend our home and countries against attack, and I suppose as long as that sort of feeling exists and until we can all truly claim to be pacifist it is probable that there will be wars. The wheel of fortune had taken a long time to turn full circle for Horst and myself and it is nice to be able to write a happy end to it — from foe to friend.

This really brings me to the end of the story of my brief war and the events that arose from it. It should be possible to draw some very deep-founded moral from it, but not being able to, I will have to leave that to any reader who has managed to get this far! As to those newspaper reporters who now and again when writing about me used the word 'Hero', would they please, if there is a next time, preface it with 'Reluctant'.

APPENDIX ONE

Summary of aircraft flown

Below are listed with their units all the aircraft flown by Major Partridge until he was taken PoW on 13th June, 1940. The sections of his log book covering the period April to June 1940 when he was commanding 800 Squadron are reproduced in facsimile at the end of this Appendix.

'Personal' aircraft are indicated by an asterisk (*).

Training — 1 FTS, RAF Leuchars September 1933 to August 1934.

A Flight — September to December 1933
Avro 504N — J9290, J9428, K1051, K1801, K1823, K1970, K1973, K1988.

B Flight — January to April 1934
Bristol Bulldog TM — K3172, K3175
Fairey Flycatcher — N9619, N9925
Hawker Hart (T) — K3058, K3144, K3155, K3158, K3744
Hawker Osprey I — S1681, S1692

C Flight — May to August 1934
Avro 504N — K1970
Fairey IIIF — S1169, S1788, S1827, S1845
Fairey Seal — K3516, K3517
Hawker Nimrod I — K2824, S1628, S1629
Hawker Osprey I — S1680

Calshot Float Plane Course — July 1934
Avro Sea Tutor — K3375
Fairey Seal — K3530, K3533

802 Fleet Fighter Squadron — September 1934 to June 1936
Avro 504N — J8759
Hawker Nimrod I — K2834*, K2836, K2837, S1581, S1615, S1616, S1629, S1632, S1634, S1637, S1638, S1639
Hawker Nimrod II — K3660
Hawker Osprey III — K3628, K3639, K3643, K3916

803 Fleet Fighter Squadron — August 1936 to May 1937
      Fairey Seal (Target Tug) — K4224
      Hawker Osprey I — K2781, K2785, S1693, S1696, S1698

Pilots Pool, Gosport — June to October 1937
      Avro 504N — K1813
      Avro Tutor — K3222, K3339, K6115, K6117
      Blackburn Shark I — K4355, K4357
      Blackburn Shark II — L2337, L2339, L2341
      Fairey Swordfish — K4190, K5996, K5997
      Hawker Nimrod II — K2909, K3654, K5056, K5057
      Hawker Osprey I — S1682, S1691
      Hawker Osprey IV — K5743
      Hawker Tomtit — K1783

Walrus Conversion Course, Calshot — October 1937
      Supermarine Walrus — K8537

802 Fleet Fighter Squadron — December 1937 to October 1938
      Fairey Swordfish — K5982
      Hawker Nimrod I — K2836, S1587, S1623
      Hawker Nimrod II — K3660*, K3661, K4627
      Hawker Osprey III — K3652, K4334

Worthy Down — May 1939
      Blackburn Shark — K5630

758 Squadron, Gosport — June to October 1939
      Blackburn Shark II — K5631, K5632, K5636, K5655, K8454, K8469,
                      K8485, K8892, L2337
      Blackburn Skua — L2907, L2909, L2911, L2912, L2914, L2915, L2916
      Hawker Osprey III — K3617, K3618, K3641, K4335
      Hawker Osprey IV — K5743, K5750

803 Squadron, RAF Wick — November 1939
      Blackburn Skua — L2874, L2881, L2887, L2889, L2904, L2905,
                      L2923, L2925, L2948

804 Squadron, Hatston — December 1939 to March 1940
      Blackburn Skua — L2999
      Gloster Gladiator II (hooked) — N2265, N2275
      Gloster Sea Gladiator — N5504, N5509, N5510, N5538, N5545

Date and Hour	Aeroplane Type and No.	Pilot	Passenger(s)	Time	Heigh
			800		
April. 1940					
2nd 1545.	Skua L.3028.	Self.	Lb. Bostock.	4.10.	
4th 1500.	" L.3025.	"	Lt. Cdr. Edwards.	.25.	
1735.	" L.3025	"	" "	.25.	
1st 0600.	" L.3025.	"	" "	2.55.	
3rd 1415.	" "	"	Lb. Bostock.	.50.	
5th 1030.	" "	"	" "	3.45.	
6th 1105.	" "	"	" "	3.00.	
7th 0730	" "	"	P.O. Cunningham	3.35.	
8th 1630.	" "	"	Lb. Bostock.	2.30.	
9th 0745.	" L.3000.	"	P.O. Cotterill.	3.00.	
10th 0515.	" L.3025.	"	Lt. Cdr. Hare.	4.30.	
5th 1845.	" L.3025.	"	Lb. Bostock	2.25.	31.30
11th 1745.	" L.3025	"	P/O. Carlyle.	2.30.	
12th 1435.	" L.3025.	"	Lb. Bostock.	4.30.	
14th 0500.	" L.3025	"	Lb. Bostock.	4.30.	
17th 0830.	" L.3025.	"	" "	4.30.	47.30

TOTAL TIME :— | 1076h 00m

Course	REMARKS

SQUADRON.

Halston Local.	Convoy Patrol.
	Halston to Wick.
	Wick to Halston.
Halston Local.	Convoy Patrol.
" "	Investigating enemy attack on ship.
" "	Convoy Patrol.
" "	" "
" "	" "
" "	" "
" "	" "

800 and 803 Attack on "Köln" class cruiser at Bergen. D/B with 500 lb. bombs. Cruiser reported sunk. One A/C (Smeaton) lost.

" "	Convoy Patrol.
" "	" "
" "	Dive bombing & front gun attack
" "	on shipping in Bergen harbour.
	" " " "

Recce: at Bergen. Landed at Sumburgh to refuel and mixed up in a c/b ground Write off.

Date and Hour	Aeroplane Type and No.	Pilot	Passenger(s)	Time	Height
20th 1040.	Shua. L. 2940.	Self.	Lb. Bostock.	.25.	
1440.	" L. 2940.	"	" "	4.35.	
23rd 0520.	" L. 2940.	"	" "	.40.	
25th 0555.	" L. 2940.	"	" "	4.20.	
26th 1416.	" L. 2940.	"	" "	2.05.	
27th 1235.	" L. 2940.	"	" "	2.45.	4.50
			Comdr: R. N.		
			Comdr (F). H.M.S. Ark Royal		

TOTAL TIME :— | 1090 | 50

Course	Remarks
Halston Lee a.P.	A/C. Test. Attack on enemy warships at Larvik. no target found. Attached M.T.B. at Bergen. Halston to Ark Royal. 138(4) Fighter patrol over Namsos area. 139(4) " " " Andalsnes 140(4) area. Attacked He. 111. Fighter patrol over Andalsnes. Attacked + shot down He. 111. Engine failed + force landed on frozen Lake at Groth. Burnt A/C.

		DAY			NIGHT		
TOTAL FLYING ALL TYPES (HOURS)		SOLO	DUAL	PASS	SOLO	DUAL	PASS
		982·25	55·25	22·05	30·55		
TYPE OF AIRCRAFT		FLYING LAST MONTH			TOTAL FLYING AT UNIT		
		SOLO	DUAL	PASS	SOLO	DUAL	PASS
SKUA		62·20	-	-	62·20	-	′
NIGHT FLYING	30·55						

Date and Hour	Aeroplane Type and No.	Pilot	Passenger(s)	Time	Height
May 1940.					
23rd 1405.	Skua. 2995	Self.	Lt. Bostock.	1.45.	2000
25th 1700.	" "	"	" "	1.05.	1,000.
		Comdr: R.N.			
		Comdr: (F) H.M.S. Ark Royal.			
June 1940.					
4th 2330.	Skua. 2995.	Self.	Lt. Bostock.	3.40.	3,000.
1115.	" "	"	" "	3.40.	3,000
6th 0200.	" "	"	" "	3.40.	
7th 0430.	" "	"	" "	3.50.	
8th 2300.	" "	"	" "	3.50.	
8th 1110.	" "	"	" "	3.05.	
9th 1540	" "	"	" "	3.20	
9th 2400	" "	"	" "	3.15	
13th 0001.	" "	Self.	" "	2.10.	
	Completed to last flight 13.6.40.				
	G.R. Callingham Lt. R.N. Squadron.				

TOTAL TIME :— 1124 h. 10 m.

Course	Remarks
	Donibristle to Halston.
	Halston to Ark Royal. 141 (48)

TOTAL FLYING ALL TYPES (HOURS)	DAY			NIGHT		
	SOLO	DUAL	PASS	SOLO	DUAL	PASS
	985.15	55.85	22.05	30.55		

TYPE OF AIRCRAFT	FLYING LAST MONTH			TOTAL FLYING AT UNIT		
	SOLO	DUAL	PASS	SOLO	DUAL	PASS
Skua.	2.50	.	.	65.10	.	.

NIGHT FLYING 30.55

Course	Remarks
Narvik.	F.P. over Transports evacuating Narvik.
"	Recce: South of Narvik.
"	F.P. over Transports evacuating Narvik.
"	" " " " "
"	F.P. over Narvik.
"	F.P. over Transports leaving Narvik.
"	" "
"	" "
Ark Royal to Trondheim.	800 & 803 Sqdns. D.B. attack on German Fleet at Trondheim. Intercepted after attack by two M.E.109s. On fire at 4000 ft. Band and + Eatie taken prisoner. Bostock killed.

This early 1937 advertisement, one of the first Blackburn released showing their new Skua aircraft, emphasizes its dive-bomber designation in this artist's impression.

The Skua's recovery

by Lieutenant Andrew G. Linsley, RN, Recovery Team Leader

In 1973 the Naval Air Command Sub Aqua Club was asked if it would mount an Expedition to Lesjaskog, in Central Norway, to look for Gladiator parts in 1974. These parts were required to assist the Fleet Air Arm Museum at Yeovilton in its efforts to restore a Sea Gladiator to display condition. It was well known that Gladiators from No 263 Squadron, RAF which had been ferried to Norway by the aircraft carrier HMS *Glorious*, lay at the bottom of Lesjaskog lake, in the valley next to Breidalsvatn.

However, in August 1973, two Norwegian divers found the remains of a Blackburn Skua Mk II in a lake at Grotli, in the next valley to Lesjaskog. As this was the only known example of this type of aircraft to date it is not difficult to understand why the emphasis was shifted to this unique 'find' fairly rapidly!

After 12 months of intensive planning and organization, coupled with the very able assistance of Charterhall Productions Ltd., the company who filmed the whole of the recovery operation as a television documentary, the project was mounted in July/August of 1974 as the annual adventure training expedition of the Sub Aqua Club.

At 17.30 on the 11th of July, 1974, the party of 25, consisting of 13 divers, six personnel from the Mobile Air Transport Salvage Unit, HMS *Daedalus*, Lee-on-Solent, and six members of the film unit, left Newcastle-on-Tyne in the MV *Jupiter*. They arrived at Bergen the next day; split into two groups for the next stage of their journey to Grotli, where they all arrived safely at 2230 on the evening of the 13th July.

They then set up in what was to be their home for the next five weeks, an austere, but comfortable for all that, Youth Hostel next door to Sevald Grotli's house, where Partridge and Bostock had been taken 34 years before. They were joined by the two Norwegian divers, who had made the discovery, and they were to work alongside the British divers for the rest of the operation.

The very next day saw the start of the reconnaissance dives and acclimatization of the divers not used to diving in water 23 metres deep, 3000 feet above sea level, and at a temperature of 1-2 degrees centigrade! The recovery team was joined by Major Partridge and he took the opportunity of having a look at the remains of 'his' Heinkel. He also met Mr Grotli whom he had not met since 1940!

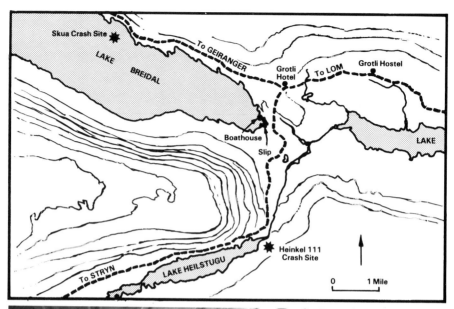

PO G A Tucker chats to film advisor Mike Rosenburg of Charterhall Films Ltd in the foyer of the Grotli Hotel.

The survey party returns from a stint — FCHEL F S Shaw, PO A J Bull, Cdr R S Lowick, Lt Linsley, and a Norwegian expert.

The engine and wings being towed to Base 1; FCHEL Shaw checks the lifting bag strops — the Skua was recovered from a depth of 24 metres.

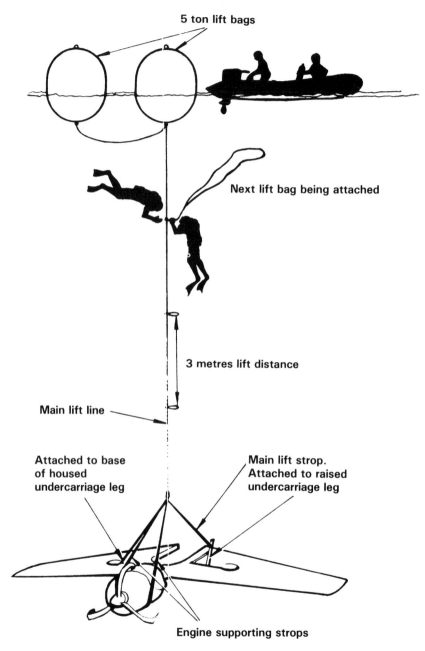

5 ton lift bags

Next lift bag being attached

3 metres lift distance

Main lift line

Attached to base of housed undercarriage leg

Main lift strop. Attached to raised undercarriage leg

Engine supporting strops

MAINPLANE & ENGINE LIFT

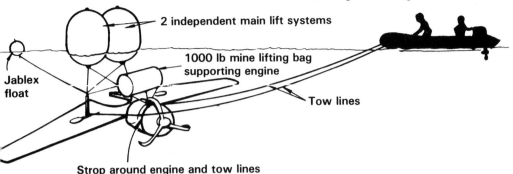

RFD 'Z' boat fitted with 20 hp Johnson outboard engine, towing astern

2 independent main lift systems

1000 lb mine lifting bag supporting engine

Jablex float

Tow lines

Strop around engine and tow lines

MAINPLANE & ENGINE SECTION UNDER TOW

On 18th July two incidents occurred which marred the whole project: CPO John Waterfield had to be flown to the Norwegian Diving School at the Naval Base, Bergen suffering from a bad attack of the 'bends'. After expert treatment, he recovered and eventually returned to HMS *Daedalus*. The same day Sevald Grotli died suddenly and the team then had the sad experience of attending a Norwegian funeral.

Meanwhile at the lake the main lifting operation of the 48 foot wing and engine section complete was achieved by the technique shown in the accompanying diagram. This section was then towed to the eastern end of the lake to a specially prepared site. The film crew then staged the discovery of the aircraft under water (once more — for the cameras) and the Tiffs and Mechs did probably one of the fastest engine removals from a Skua on record — it took them only 30 minutes to get it off!

A slipway had been constructed with the aid of a Norwegian bulldozer driver with a liking for good Scotch whisky with the Black Gang moving underwater obstacles. The engine was the first to come ashore by means of the specially constructed sledge-cum-cradle which MARTSU had brought with them from England. The wing section did not prove to be so easy: one of the two main spars had been burnt through by the fire in 1940; the second could not stand the weight imposed on it and broke. It was, therefore, divided and the separate sections lifted out by means of the HIAB crane fitted to the seven ton lorry. All this had taken roughly two weeks, so the divers took a 'rest cure' by diving in the comparatively warm water of Giranger fjord. The project leader tried an abortive resupply of gin from the *Queen Elizabeth II* which happened to be visiting the fjord on that day.

By this time the half-way stage had been reached, and this was marked by the arrival of a Heron aircraft of 781 Squadron at Alesund. It brought a change-over of eight divers and the President of NACSAC, Captain A.P. Comrie RN, who had come

The Skua engine — mounted on its recovery sledge — after being towed out, near the boathouse at the eastern end of the lake, for post immersion treatment by MARTSU.

to see at first hand what the Wombles of Grotli were up to. The fact that he was a trustee of the Museum at Yeovilton might have had something to do with his visit! The Phase 1 divers left, with Captain Comrie, the next day, and Phase 2 were initiated into the delights of diving 'in iced gin, — without the 'gin'!

From the experience gained during the first half it did not take the second team very long to raise and recover the 15 feet of rear fuselage and tail that still remained at the bottom of the lake. They then completed the Wombling of both the deep and shallow sites which had been used during the recovery. They found many small and interesting parts of the aircraft, including both the clocks, one complete with its second hand.

15th August saw the arrival at Stryn of HMAV *Audener,* a Landing Ship (Tank) belonging to the Royal Corps of Transport, which had come from England to bring

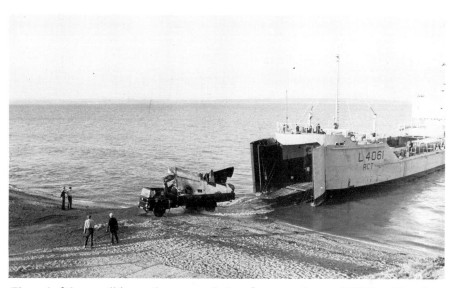

The end of the expedition — the recovered aircraft comes ashore at HMS *Daedalus* after 34 years immersion ...

... and the author takes a closer look at the remains of the wing section.

both L2940 and her recovery team home. She off-loaded a Task Trailer and Bedford KGA tug-unit which came up to Grotli, where it was loaded with the aircraft and equipment. In the meantime one party of divers had gone up to Trondheim to help recover a Heinkel He 111 and Messerschmitt 109E for the Imperial War Museum. A second team of divers spent three days at Lesjaskog in an effort to recover any bits of Gladiator worth having, but their search was in vain.

On 20th August the transport made the perilous descent to Stryn with the whole party and aircraft, where they were loaded into *Audener*. The ship finally left for England on the 22nd, but not before the project leader had taken delivery of two of the wing guns which the Norwegians had removed way back in 1940. The cost — three bottles of whisky!

At 07.30 on the morning of 27th August 1974 Blackburn Skua L2940 came ashore at HMS *Daedalus* after 34 years in Norway. Volunteers at HMS *Daedalus* spent a further twelve months cleaning and refurbishing the aircraft for display.

The Skua was finally delivered to the Fleet Air Arm Museum on 13th April 1975 and was carefully placed on the floor with its wheels retracted as it had come to rest on the ice 35 years earlier.

This advertisement appeared in 1939.

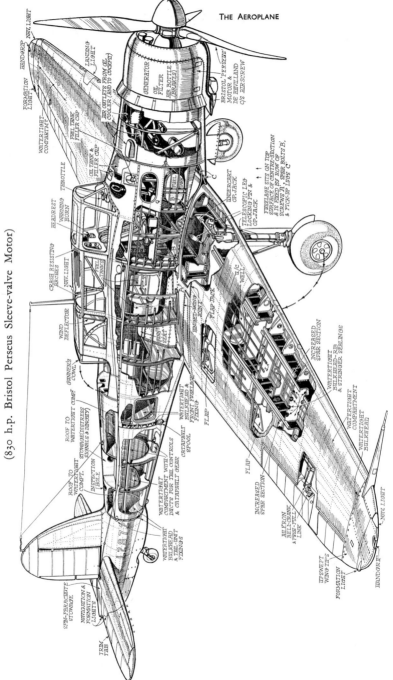

THE AEROPLANE

THE BLACKBURN SKUA FIGHTER DIVE-BOMBER
(830 h.p. Bristol Perseus Sleeve-valve Motor)

NAV. LIGHT

HANDGRIP

FORMATION LIGHT

LANDING-LIGHT

WATERTIGHT COMPARTMENT

AIR OUTLETS FROM OIL COOLER (AND TO COCKPIT)

FUEL TANK FILLER CAP

OIL TANK & FILLER CAP

GENERATOR

OIL FILTER

AIR BOTTLE (BRAKES)

BRISTOL "PERSEUS" MOTOR & DE HAVILLAND C/S AIRSCREW

THROTTLE

HEADREST

WARNING HORN

UNDERCART OP. JACK

TELESCOPIC LEG-LOCKING PIN & OP. JACK

FUSELAGE SITS ON TOP SURFACE OF CENTRE-SECTION & IS FIXED BY ROW OF SCREWS "A", SPAR BOLTS "B", & PICK-UP LUGS "C"

CRASH RESISTING ARCHES

NAV. LIGHT

FUEL TANKS

INCREASED SPAR SECTION

WIND DEFLECTOR

HINGED WING JOINT

U/C WELL

FLAP JACK

WATERTIGHT BULKHEAD & STRINGER SEALINGS

WATERTIGHT COMPARTMENT BULKHEAD

GUNNER'S COWL

WATERTIGHT BULKHEAD & FRONT FUSELAGE FIXING

FLAP

WATERTIGHT BULKHEAD-RIB

ROOF TO WATERTIGHT COMPT.

STOWAGE FOR DISTRESS SIGNALS & DINGHY

INSPECTION HOLE

CATAPULT SPOOL

FLAP

INCREASED SPAR SECTION

ROOF TO WATERTIGHT COMPT.

WATERTIGHT COMPARTMENT WITH DUCTS FOR TAIL CONTROLS & CATAPULT GEAR

AILERON BELL-CRANK & PUSH-PULL LINK

UPSWEPT WING-TIP'S

FORMATION LIGHT

HANDGRIP

NAV. LIGHT

WATERTIGHT BULKHEAD & TAIL-UNIT FIXINGS

SPIN-PARACHUTE STOWAGE

NAVIGATION & FORMATION LIGHTS

TRIM TAB

APPENDIX THREE

Blackburn Skua described

Blackburn aircraft have been supplied for Naval use since the very early days of the Fleet's association with the Air Arm. The latest Blackburn-built and Blackburn-designed aeroplane to be supplied to the Fleet Air Arm, the Blackburn Skua, is the first monoplane to be adopted for that purpose. It is also the first two-seat fighter dive-bomber for the Navy.

The Skua is primarily designed for use from aircraft carriers. So its wings have to fold. The ingenious way in which this requirement has been met, in spite of the difficulties imposed by combining it with the installation of a retractable undercarriage, deserves special mention.

Another feature of the Skua, imposed by operational requirements, are the special flaps. They are a modification of the Zapp type, in that the upper edge slides back as the flap is lowered. These flaps are placed just behind the rear spar. They not only improve the take-off and steepen the glide but can be lowered to limit speed when diving. The design is such that even when the flaps are lowered at very high flying speeds there is little change of trim.

To provide buoyancy in the event of forced descent onto water, various water-tight compartments are provided in the wings and in the fuselage. Also the cockpit itself is water-tight up to the coaming.

The distinctive arrangement of the fin and tailplane is, no doubt, to ensure the best possible measure of control, particularly in spins.

Equipment: As a two-seater fighter the Skua has fixed machine-guns in the leading edge of the wings, firing forward outside the airscrew disc, and one movable machine-gun on a special mounting at the back of the cockpit. The fixed machine-guns are controlled conventionally from the pilot's cockpit. For practice or training purposes, a camera-gun may be mounted on the starboard side of the centre section and be operated by the same control as the machine-guns.

Provision is made in the rear of the cockpit for radio transmitting and receiving apparatus with fixed and trailing aerials; for electrical services, including navigation and identification lamps, landing lamps, and the like; for marine equipment, including an inflatable dinghy, marine distress signals, slinging gear, and so on; and for miscellaneous equipment including fire extinguisher, oxygen apparatus and parachutes.

Accommodation: The crew is accommodated in a long enclosed cockpit with a transparent cover. The pilot is over the centre section and has an excellent outlook in all directions, especially for the approach when alighting. Access to the pilot's seat is gained by a sliding hood which may be locked in open, closed and intermediate positions. The windscreen is specially designed to give clear vision in wet weather and also to prevent draught in the cockpit when the sliding hood is open. A controllable cockpit heating system is provided and the pilot's seat is adjustable for height.

The observer-gunner is well aft of the wings and is provided with a fixed seat from which to work the radio. A hinged hood encloses the aft end of the cockpit and a well in the fuselage decking houses the machine-gun when not in use. The cabin enclosure has sliding side-panels, which, when opened, operate wind-deflectors that prevent the slipstream from entering the cockpit.

The pilot's windscreen is specially strengthened. Also two of the fuselage frames behind the pilot's seat are extended up to the cabin roof to stiffen the superstructure and form a protection for the crew in the event of the aeroplane turning over on the ground.

Design and Construction: The fuselage is a metal monococque structure in two sections joined just forward of the fun. Alclad frames, stringers and special sections riveted together, carry flush-riveted plating. Two water-tight compartments are built into the main structure, one forward under the pilot's floor and the other aft behind the cockpit.

The detachable after section of the fuselage structure is of similar construction to the main structure to which it is bolted. It carries the tail unit and tail wheel and has light metal fairings for the tail wheel and to complete the lines of the tailplane.

Wings: The wings are built in three sections, the centre section, and two outer planes. The centre section is detachable. It is bolted under the fuselage so that its upper surface forms the bottom of the front water-tight compartment of the fuselage.

The centre section structure comprises two main box-spars composed of Alclad-plate webs reinforced by vertical stiffeners and flanges of extruded section, flanged-plate ribs, Z-section stringers and plating riveted with flush and hollow rivets.

The outer planes taper both in plan and thickness and have detachable up-swept tips. The construction is similar to that of the centre-section except that the main girders are of box-section over part of their length from the wing-root but change to a single web towards the wing-tip. Water-tight compartments are provided between the main girders forward of the ailerons.

Near the wing-root a circular recess for the undercarriage wheel, and troughs for the struts, are let into the undersurface of each outer plane. Forward of the trailing edge and between the aileron and the wing-root is a trough wherin are housed the wing-flap which stows flush with the undersurface of the wing when not in use. The flaps are metal-framed and metal-covered.

The ailerons have inset hinges and ball bearings. They have a single girder-type spar, reinforced by a metal leading edge, and ribs pressed from Alclad sheet. The covering is fabric.

Tail Unit: The fixed tail-plane is a cantilever and is bolted to two frames of the rear portion of the fuselage. The tail-plane has two girder spars, formers and transverse Z-section stringers. The metal plating is riveted on with hollow rivets.

The elevators have inset-hinges and trimming tabs with irreversible controls operated from the cockpit. The elevators are interconnected by means of a cross-shaft. The framework consists of single girder spars, Alclad formers and leading edges. The covering is fabric. All hinges are ball bearings.

The cantilever fin is detachable from the fuselage. It is a metal-covered structure, which comprises an Alclad sternpost, sternpost bracing strut, flanged formers and flanged leading-edge formers. The plating is secured by hollow rivets.

The rudder, of similar construction to the elevators, has a horn-balance and inset hinges. The balance-tab operates automatically. The trimming-tab has irreversible controls operated from the cockpit. All hinges are ball bearings.

Undercarriage: The undercarriage retracts outwards and upwards into recesses in the outer main planes. The wheels have intermediate pressure tyres and pneumatic brakes.

Each unit consists of an oleo-pneumatic shock-absorber strut with stub-axle and wheel, a rear stay and a telescopic side stay. The shock-absorber strut and rear stay hinge about the same fore and aft axis and the telescopic strut is hinged between and inboard of these struts.

Each strut has a light metal fairing which, when the undercarriage is retracted, fairs the under surface of the main plane.

To the top of the shock absorber strut is bolted a lever which extends above the hinge-centre. This lever is coupled to a hydraulic jack which raises and lowers the undercarriage.

Locking devices, also operated by hydraulic jacks, are to secure the undercarriage in both the raised and lowered positions. Each lock operates an electrical indicator which shows, by illumination of coloured lamps in the cockpit, the position of the lock. A mechanical indicator in the wing and visible from the cockpit also shows the position of each undercarriage unit. Electrical, visual and audible warning indicators are incorporated in the system.

The tail-wheel unit comprises a coiled shock absorber strut with castored fork and electrically conductive tyre. The springing of the shock-absorber strut is oil-damped. In the air the wheel is maintained in a fore-and-aft position by a self-centring device in the strut.

Flying Controls: The control surfaces are operated by a normal system of cables, pulleys and levers. The control-column has a knuckle-joint so that lateral movement of the upper portion controls the ailerons.

From the upper portion of the control column two chains are taken down the column over sprockets to tie-rods connected to the horizontal arms of a three-armed lever mounted on the forward wall of the bomb compartment. Cables from the vertical arm of the lever are conducted by pulleys down the centre line of each main-plane hinge-joint into the main planes to levers linked to the leading edge of the ailerons. A balance-cable connects both ailerons.

From the lower portion of the control-column, which is supported in ball bearings, a control rod is taken to the elevator cross-shaft. From a lever on the port end of the cross-shaft, cables are led down the port side of the fuselage in a water-tight duct to a lever on the intermediate portion of the elevator spar. A second lever on the spar is connected by a link rod to a mass balance arm installed in the fuselage.

The rudder-bar is adjustable by means of a central star-wheel which, when rotated, moves the extremities of the rudder bar backward or forward. The pedals are pivoted and have parallel motion. Two pairs of cables are attached to a lever on the rudder bar spindle. Each pair is taken over pulleys on the port and starboard sides of the cockpit, down the sides of the fuselage, to a lever on the rudder-post.

The trimming-tabs for the elevator and rudder are operated by two handwheels mounted on the port side of the cockpit. The larger handwheel operates the elevator-tabs. Chains are taken from these handwheels to a countershaft mounted on the pilot's floor. From sprockets and chains on the starboard end of the countershaft, cables are led down the starboard side of the fuselage to similar chain and sprocket gear.

These sprockets incorporate the nuts for screw gear which adjusts each trimmer control through a countershaft and rod and lever system. Position indicators for the trimming tabs are mounted in the cockpit.

The Power Plant: The power unit is a Bristol Perseus XII air-cooled, sleeve-valve, radial engine fitted with a controllable pitch three-bladed airscrew. It provides 830 hp for take-off and is rated at 745 hp at 2,400 rpm at 6,500 feet. It is cowled by a fairing ring, and the cooling is controlled by gills.

The engine mounting is a tubular two-bay structure bolted to attachment fittings on the fuselage front bulkhead which carries a mounting ring. Aft of the fairing ring the mounting is enclosed by detachable cowl panels. All components of the installation are easily accessible.

There are two main tanks in the sides of the cockpit and a smaller reserve tank in the front water-tight compartment. Fuel is fed to the motor by engine-driven pump through selector cocks so that fuel can be taken from any tank, or combination of tanks. A damaged tank or its pipe line may be isolated from the remainder of the system.

Each tank is fitted with an electrical contents gauge, drain plug, air vent, and a special trap to retain fuel at the supply pipe during diving manoeuvres of the aeroplane. All tanks are readily removable.

The oil is carried in a 12-gallon tank mounted in the fuselage decking immediately in front of the pilot's instrument panel. The tank contains a partial circulating chamber with a regulator, adjustable on the ground, to suit different climatic conditions.

Incorporated in the pressure-pump is an automatic oil-pressure device which allows cold oil, by-passed by the relief valve, to build up a pressure adequate for the lubrication of all bearings when the motor is started from cold.

The oil-cooler, mounted internally on the engine mounting, has two forward-facing air ducts. A manifold, which has three ducts, is at the back of the cooler; the two outer ducts are led to atmosphere, but the middle duct, in which is incorporated a shutter, is led to the pilot's cockpit. When warm air is not wanted in the cockpit, the shutter may be operated to deflect the warm air into the two outer ducts.

The system also includes an oil-cleaner, carburetter heating jacket, drain plugs and thermometer pockets, all of which are easily accessible.

The aero-motor is started by a cartridge starter electrically fired. The pistol unit is mounted on the port side of the cockpit and is connected by a pipe line to the turbine unit mounted on the back of the motor. The latter is primed by the normal priming system.

Hydraulic and Pneumatic Systems: The hydraulic system operates the retractable undercarriage units and the flaps on the wings. It comprises an engine-driven pump, fluid reservoir, main and emergency selector-valves, restrictor-valves and hydraulic jacks. The selector-valve has separate control valves and levers for the operation of the undercarriage and that of the flaps. When the levers are in the neutral position, the fluid is circulated by the pump from the reservoir and through a bypass back to the reservoir without pressure.

When the undercarriage selector-valve lever is put to 'undercarriage up' or 'undercarriage down' the bypass is closed, the fluid passes into the pipe lines selected, pressure is built up and the jack connected to the undercarriage strut is operated. At the same time, restrictor valves in the circuit ensure that the locking devices operate appropriately before and after movement of the undercarriage.

A hand-pump is provided for use in the event of failure of the engine-driven pump or on occasions when the aero-motor is not running. The hand-pump has two deliveries, one through the normal system and the other through an emergency system. The normal system operates through the main selector-valve-box in the same way as the engine-driven pump system. The emergency system consists of a supplementary pipe line to each jack in the undercarriage system and can be used only to lower the undercarriage units.

Each wing flap is operated by a hydraulic jack mounted between the inner flap runners in the main planes. The jacks are connected by pipe lines to the main selector-valve-box which has a separate control valve and lever. A flow-control valve is introduced into the system to form a hydraulic lock for any position of the flaps.

The flaps may therefore be set at any angle, in this way the main system is relieved of the high pressure set up by the flaps in the 'down' position at high speeds. As with the undercarriage, either the engine-driven pumps or the hand-pump may be used.

A hydraulic flap position indicator is in the cockpit.

The pneumatic system comprises an engine-driven compressor, air reservoir, oil reservoir and trap, air filter and pressure gauge. A charging union is also connected to the main system to charge the reservoir from external sources. The wheel-brake system is controlled by a hand lever on the pilot's control column, the braking pressure varying according to the movement applied to the hand lever. For parking purposes the lever can be locked in position.

The relay valve, which is operated by the hand-lever, is also linked to the rudder-bar with the result that movement of the rudder-bar has a differential effect on the braking.

A single press button on the top of the pilot's control column controls the firing of the four fixed machine-guns.

Dimensions: — In flying attitude; Span, 46ft 2ins (14.07m); chord, 9ft 3ins (2.82m); length 35ft 7ins (11.45m); height over mast, 14ft 2ins (4.31m); track, 9ft 7ins (2.92m). Tail-wheel on ground: Length 34ft 10¼ins (10.62m); height over mast, 12ft 6ins (3.81m).

Areas: — Wing area, 312 sq ft (28.9sq m); flaps, 18.5 sq ft (1.7 sq m); tail-plane, 49 sq ft (4.5 sq m); elevators, 24 sq ft (2.2 sq m); fin, 9.7 sq ft (0.9 sq m); rudder, 9.9 sq ft (0.9 sq m).

Weights: *Dive-Bomber* — No particulars.
Two-Seat Fighter — Weight empty, 5,490lb (2,490kg); oil (10 gallons (45.5 litres)), 90lb (41kg).
Drogue-Target-Tower — Weight empty, 5,490lb (2,490kg); military load, 1,381lb (626kg); oil (6 gallons (27.3 litres)), 54lb (25kg).

Performance: *Dive-Bomber* — No particulars.
Two-Seat Fighter — Max speed at 6,500 feet, 225mph (362kph at 1,980m); max speed at sea level, 204mph (329kph); landing speed, 75mph (121kph); service ceiling, 20,200 feet (6,160m); max cruising speed at 15,000 feet (4,570m), 144mph (232kph).
Drogue-Target-Tower — Max speed, 229mph (360kph); max speed at sea level, 205mph (330kph); landing-speed, 68mph (109kph); service-ceiling, 22,800 feet (6,950m); economic cruising speed at 15,000 feet (4,570m); 145mph (233kph).

Index

*(Figures in **bold type** refer to illustrations or captions)*

Review your

THE FLEET AIR ARM MUSEUM, one of the world's **....it's Exciting,** major aviation museums, is tremendous entertainment and a great day out for the whole family. It contains over 40 historic military aircraft, the largest collection under one roof in Europe; in Concorde Hall stands Concorde 002; there are hundreds of models, photographs, paintings, uniforms, medals, weapons, trophies and special exhibitions that present a complete picture of the development of naval aviation from mans earliest attempts to fly, right up to the Falklands Campaign. Outside, on weekdays you can watch today's flying Navy in action with Sea Harrier Jump Jets and helicopters, because the Royal Naval Air Station Yeovilton is an active airfield with up to 500 movements a day.

FALKLANDS CAMPAIGN EXHIBITION
- *ABSORBING*

This is the most comprehensive Falklands Exhibition in the UK and includes: 'Humphrey' the shrapnel riddled Wessex 3 helicopter that fatally crippled the Argentinian submarine 'Santa Fe'; a Wasp helicopter from HMS Endurance; an Argentinian 'Pucara'; twin engined ground attack aircraft and Iroquois helicopter; a wide variety of captured weapons, equipment and relics, supported by photographs, paintings and displays telling the Fleet Air Arm's vital role in the campaign.

MODERN NAVY EXHIBITION

A special exhibition showing the high technology navy at work in the 1980's.

Review your Flying Navy for a great day out.